INTANGIBLE CAPITAL

INTANGIBLE CAPITAL

Putting Knowledge to Work in the
21st-Century Organization

MARY ADAMS AND MICHAEL OLEKSAK
Foreword by Leif Edvinsson

PRAEGER

AN IMPRINT OF ABC-CLIO, LLC
Santa Barbara, California • Denver, Colorado • Oxford, England

Library of Congress Cataloging-in-Publication Data

Oleksak, Mary Adams, 1959–
    Intangible capital : putting knowledge to work in the 21st-century organization / Mary Adams and Michael Oleksak ; foreword by Leif Edvinsson.
        p. cm.
    Includes bibliographical references and index.
    ISBN 978-0-313-38074-7 (hard copy : alk. paper)—ISBN 978-0-313-38075-4 (ebook)
1. Intellectual capital—Management. I. Oleksak, Michael M., 1957– II. Title.
    HD53.O44   2010
    658.4′038—dc22   2010000833

ISBN: 978-0-313-38074-7
EISBN: 978-0-313-38075-4

14 13 12 11 10   1 2 3 4 5

This book is also available on the World Wide Web as an eBook.
Visit www.abc-clio.com for details.

Praeger
An Imprint of ABC-CLIO, LLC

ABC-CLIO, LLC
130 Cremona Drive, P.O. Box 1911
Santa Barbara, California 93116-1911

This book is printed on acid-free paper ∞

Manufactured in the United States of America

This book is dedicated to Harroll H. Adams,
an accountant who understood the value of intangibles
and who always believed in this endeavor.

We wish you were here to share it.

c|o|n|t|e|n|t|s

foreword

In the 1980s, the global economy began to shift dramatically. Fueled by information technology, the investment by the major economies became concentrated in software, process, and knowledge, all considered "soft" and invisible—intangible—in accounting systems.

Yet, intangibles investment is at the root of the growth of our economies. I first used the concept of intangibles as the roots of a tree in my 1997 book with Michael Malone. I continue to use it in my practice of Intellectual Capital Leadership to express that intangibles, although invisible, provide the foundation for the rest of the organization in the 21st century—and fuel corporate earnings. The tree and the Legos that the authors use in this book are representations of the holistic perspective that is necessary for understanding the ecosystem of intangible capital (IC).

Beginning in the 1990s, there has been a greater effort in many countries at making the roots of our economy—intangibles—visible by creating IC reporting. The Wissenbilanz in Germany, RICARDIS and InCaS by the EU, work by METI in Japan, and efforts in Hong Kong and China have all endeavored to spread the promise of IC as a way of empowering companies to use intangibles to fuel innovation. Broad partnerships represented by the World Intellectual Capital Initiative (WICI) have united the public and private sectors on research and development of new intangibles standards. Although represented in WICI, the United States has not developed its own approach to intangibles to date.

Despite all these efforts and the great progress by interested academics and business and government leaders, the ideas and the power of IC has not yet moved into the business mainstream. That is why I am very heartened by this new work from Mary Adams and Michael Oleksak. This book is a pioneering work with an innovative way of explaining IC. It is excellent reading material with illustrative learning cases. The focus on monetization of knowledge products and services is very inspiring. The worksheets at the end of each chapter are a very practicable approach. It has a good theoretical base, building on the work of Professor Paul Romer and the New Growth Theory. The book has many helpful distinctions on human capital, relational capital, and organizational structural capital, as well as intellectual property.

I can strongly recommend this for not only reading but also application. It is timely and interesting for business as well as the G 20 leaders as we move out of the global recession.

Leif Edvinsson

The World's First Director of Intellectual Capital
The World's First Professor of Intellectual Capital

preface

We have lived the transition from the industrial to the knowledge era in real time. We were both educated during the 1960s and 1970s. We used our first PCs as young professionals in the early 1980s. We started our careers in banking, went through training programs, and learned to size commercial loans against the assets on our customers' balance sheets. We both remember when the assets began to fall short of the amount of money needed for a new loan or a leveraged buyout (as private equity deals were called then). As we moved through our careers, we experienced firsthand the growing computerization of every kind of work. And many of the business skills and tools we learned early in our careers failed to provide answers to the challenges we and our clients faced.

When we started a consulting firm 11 years ago, many of the financial skills we developed as bankers fell short in explaining what was going on inside our clients' businesses. We created our own approaches to figuring out what was going on. Then, five years ago, we received an e-mail from a company called Intellectual Capital Sweden. That e-mail set us on a learning journey. Through our colleagues in Sweden, especially Henrik Martin and Peder Hofman-Bang, we learned a new vocabulary and a new way of looking at companies.

We joined the international network of companies that license IC Rating, a tool developed in Sweden which is today owned by Actcell in Japan. Through our interaction with this network and the broader global IC community, we entered the world of intangible capital. This book reflects how we have learned to apply the ideas of intangible capital to solving questions of how to grow, deal with change, and build long-term value in our clients' companies.

There have been a lot of people who have helped us along the way. Ken Lizotte and Jeff Olson believed in this project and saw it through to the end. Henrik and Peder introduced us to Leif Edvinsson, who, along with Karl-Erik Sveiby and Thomas A. Stewart, was one of the earliest thinkers in the field. Other long-time leaders in the field, Verna Allee and Debra Amidon, have been very supportive and helpful. Our colleagues at the Intangible Asset Finance Society, especially fearless leader Nir Kossovsky, have shared their time and knowledge. Ken Jarboe at the Athena Alliance has been an ally in translating the wonderful work done all over the world for the American psyche. Michael Kimbrough at Harvard Business School helped us bridge the worlds of accounting and IC. David Phillips and the team at the PricewaterhouseCoopers Corporate Reporting Group have been generous to us and to the field, sharing their knowledge openly and never giving up on the goal of finding a way for accountants to be part of the intangibles solution.

All these people and many more helped us with early critiques of this book. Henrik Martin and Ken Jarboe both gave thorough reads to drafts of this book. We benefited from a spirited discussion on the lines between intellectual property and other knowledge with Neil Wilkof, Jordan Hatcher, Jackie Hutter, and many thoughtful folks who commented on Mary's blog. Many of our colleagues are mentioned in the pages that follow. This field is still emerging and we all continue to learn from each other. Our goal with this book is to broaden the conversation, put more ideas to work, and bring our readers into the discussion, too, through our Web site.

Our country and our world has been handed many challenges caused, you could say, by the lack of sustainability in the industrial economic model. But we are facing these challenges with a whole new set of tools and knowledge fueled by information technology and the rise of the knowledge era. We look forward to working with you to put that knowledge to work and fuel a new era of prosperity.

Mary Adams
Michael Oleksak

introduction

What if one day your phone rings, and it's a colleague who wants to talk with you about a company. This company has been around for decades and has grown steadily in recent years. It has good people. Although it has had a rough time in the last recession, it is holding its own and believes that it will be able to benefit from a strengthening economy. Its market holds promise of innovation and growth. Would you take the call? Does this sound interesting enough that you would recommend a deeper look as a potential partner, investor, board member, or employee?

What if, on closer examination, you discovered that the company has a production facility that it started piecing together in the 1980s with internally built components? Occasionally, the owners bought third-party parts but, by and large, even these were customized to the point that they are unique to the company. This facility started as a little experiment but has come to be one of the company's most important competitive advantages. Some would say it is *the* competitive advantage of the company.

When you ask about this facility, you find that since it grew from the inside out, the company never brought it into their accounting. It has no inventory of its raw materials or its production assets. It doesn't keep track of how much it cost to build, maintain, and operate the facility. It doesn't have a map of the production flow of its operations. Would you still have the same opinion? Would you recommend a relationship with this company? Or would you be concerned about the quality of its management, its ability to continue to generate earnings, even the long-term viability of the company?

These are really important questions because the company we are describing is the company where you work, the companies in your retirement plan, the companies on which the United States is banking its future. Our economy has made a fundamental shift from industrial to knowledge production. We still manufacture goods (although less than in the past). But the basis of competition has shifted. Competitive advantage is now based on what you *know* rather than what you *own*.

Every company today has an invisible production facility, a knowledge factory, where it converts raw knowledge into scalable and repeatable processes that create value for its customers. This factory is there whether you manufacture physical goods or you provide a service. Knowledge, fueled by information technology, is the raw material, the fuel, and the engine of this factory. The success of your company is totally dependent on the success of this knowledge factory.

Yet very few companies can provide a description of their own knowledge factory. Nor can they provide an inventory of its critical components. How much it cost to build, maintain, and operate the factory. How well it is performing. The knowledge factory is essentially invisible in most companies.

Experts estimate that easily half, probably much more, of the value of American companies is held in this knowledge factory. This factory has been built through steady investments that were at least equal to the investments made in tangible production capacity in recent decades—and probably much greater. The future of your company and our country will depend on our ability to leverage this investment. But neither the investment nor the value of this knowledge factory is captured in the accounting and management information systems that are used across our economy. And the exclusion of intangibles also means that the operating story that accounting has traditionally told—as raw material moves through the production process and becomes finished goods—is also missing. Today's accounting shows very little balance sheet movement and a lot of different kinds of expenses, both tangible and intangible, but no coherent story about the value creation process.

All this means that managers, boards of directors, investors, partners, and stakeholders of all kinds have to rely on their intuition to evaluate the creation, strength, and monetization of intangibles. They ask questions, they get a gut feel for how things work. But they do not get hard data that give them a complete picture of the current and future productive knowledge capacity of our companies.

This is the dangerous secret of our economy. We have all kinds of regulations about corporate disclosure. We have all kinds of management practices vetted by business schools. We profess to value hard data. But no company today can provide a basic set of management information on its knowledge assets and the means by which these assets are put to work to create customer value. And no one will admit that they are managing by depending on their intuition.

And now we are at a moment of truth. Our economy seemingly made huge progress in the past decades. Computers created efficiencies and fueled profits. They also enabled many white collar jobs to be moved off shore along with manufacturing work. The economic consequences of this outsourcing and the mothballing of so much of our economic infrastructure were hidden by a series of economic booms in the 1990s and early 2000s. Then the "Great Recession" of 2008–2009 exposed the fact that our economy was running on consumer spending fueled by financial profits that have long since disappeared. Today, we lack sources of job creation and true economic growth. Add to this economic challenge the even greater ones created by serious concerns about our environment, our energy use, our health care system, even our food production. We are in a very difficult position.

What will it take to face these challenges? How can we as a nation convert these enormous challenges into opportunities that can fuel a new century of growth and prosperity? The answers lie in how we leverage the enormous intangible capital of American business. The seeds of the future already exist in the minds of our workers and in the collection of knowledge—the intangible capital—of our organizations. But we are not going to rise to these challenges by ignoring this same intangible capital in our management information and practices. We must use our intangible capital, not to re-create the past but to create a new future.

The times, the challenges, and the opportunities demand that we develop intangibles management capabilities to move almost every sector of our economy into the knowledge era to:

- Re-create manufacturing in a new knowledge-intensive and sustainable form.
- Change energy production and use across our entire economy.
- Create a sustainable, healthy food system.
- Re-think education at every level.
- Use our greatest resource—our collective knowledge—to fuel a new era of prosperity.

We are both former bankers who began our careers just as the IBM PC hit the marketplace in the early 1980s. That was actually the moment when a discernable "extra" value became visible in the public markets over and above the book value of corporate assets. In hindsight, economists now tell us that this was when the knowledge era began to take off. We, like all businesspeople today, have lived with feet planted in both the industrial and knowledge eras. At Citibank and Bank of Boston, we each received training in state-of-the-art business thinking. But as time went by, it became clear that there was something else going on. The old formulae didn't work. Assets wouldn't cover the loan amounts companies needed to fund their operations. It was only later when we had started a consulting firm in the late 1990s that we came to understand the shift that was under way.

Then, over five years ago, we were introduced to the emerging field of intangible capital. We started an informational Web site, the IC Knowledge Center (ICKC), and a newsletter that became our way of continuing (and sharing) our learning. The ICKC later morphed into a blog and as of early 2010 became a network with participants from many fields of expertise from all over the globe. We also began to apply the concepts in our client work, helping technology and service companies to grow and adapt to changes in their markets. We began to see a lot of trends that have been emerging in recent years—social networking, innovation, performance, and knowledge management—as threads of the same story. Eventually we felt compelled to write a book to pull all these threads together.

This is not the first book we have written together. We met and lived in the Dominican Republic over 20 years ago. At the time we were intrigued by the growing prominence of Latin Americans in baseball. We were upset when we would see sportswriters speculate (often incorrectly) on how and why baseball spread to different countries. When we couldn't find a book on the rich history of this aspect of our national game, we decided to write it ourselves. We helped set the record straight and start a new thread in the history of baseball.

This book isn't all that different. We have shared with our clients the urgency of being able to measure, manage, and monetize intangibles. We have seen what works. But we haven't been able to find a book that explains this in a clear, practical way. We felt we had no choice but to do it ourselves. Our hope is to get this information out to a broader audience and contribute to the important conversation about how to stimulate innovation and growth in our economy.

The ideas we express here are grounded in the best and most current research. But everything is filtered through the lens of our experience—and that of our clients—as to what really works. Our goal is to arm you with understanding and perhaps more importantly, practical tools and applications to help your organization succeed in the knowledge era. Each idea is linked with its industrial-era equivalent so that you can see where it fits in your daily work.

There are three major parts of the book. The New Factory focuses on the performance of your intangible capital. The New Management is about driving innovation in your organization. And the New Accounting explains the link between intangibles and the financial performance and valuation of your business. These images and concepts describe the knowledge-era equivalents of familiar basics in business. We are not advocating the abandonment of the existing basics but, rather, supplementing your existing practices with new ones better suited to the knowledge side of your business.

The New Factory introduces knowledge as a business asset. It's actually a very flexible asset and can take many forms: as a product, as a raw material, and as an engine for the growth of your company. This part explains the economics of getting paid for knowledge (and sometimes giving it away) and how knowledge becomes a raw material for your business through three basic classes of assets: human, relationship, and structural knowledge capital. You'll learn that structural capital is the most powerful knowledge asset because it is infinitely scalable and repeatable. But that in order to use and monetize any of these assets, they need to be combined in a system, what we call the knowledge factory. We'll show you how to build a model of your knowledge factory that will help you in thinking about how to measure, manage, and maximize the performance of your organization's knowledge.

The New Management introduces the layers of networks that make up the knowledge factory and that limit the usefulness of traditional management tools like organization charts, strategic planning, and managerial controls. By definition, knowledge is spread throughout your knowledge factory. That means that you need to learn to "manage" information flows from the bottom up and outside in. Nowhere is this more necessary than in the area of innovation where your challenge is to facilitate the development and implementation of new ideas from all levels of your organization as well as your customers and external partners.

The New Accounting explains how today's businessperson is hampered by lack of information about the knowledge factory. Knowledge assets are not captured in accounting systems and are almost invisible in other conventional forms of management information. We will introduce you to strategies to remedy this situation through the creation of simple reports about the cost, strength, and performance of your knowledge factory. You can use these reports immediately to support your internal management. We will also prepare you for the day when you use this kind of information to communicate with external stakeholders including investors, bankers, partners, customers, and even employees to increase the valuation that they assign to your business. We end by explaining how your reputation is dependent on the success of the management of your knowledge factory. It holds your factory network together and ensures that your factory will be able to grow and innovate heading into the future.

It is this possibility of performance, innovation, and valuation that we hope will lead you to adapt your thinking and your management approaches to the knowledge era. To this end, you will find an exercise at the end of each chapter that will help shape your thinking and apply its lessons in your own company. There is a companion Web site to this book, www.intangiblecapitalbook.com, where you can download worksheets for all these exercises as well as guides for how these ideas can be best exploited by different business functions: the CEO, CFO, CIO, COO, IP, and HR professionals inside a company as well as investment, finance, and legal professionals who advise companies from the outside. Through the Web site, we hope to stimulate a conversation to build on the ideas presented here. The really important ideas are yet to come. And they will come from the millions of managers on the ground who live in real time the challenges of living at the intersection between the industrial and knowledge eras. We can all learn from each other and speed the creation of a new management model.

We see the current challenges facing our clients and companies across the globe as once-in-a-lifetime opportunities to create wealth and well-being. The answer is in the knowledge you already have and the knowledge that you can create through collaboration with the participants in your knowledge factory. We thank you for joining us on this journey.

The New Factory

Knowledge is *the* critical resource in today's economy. Business success and growth today are dependent on knowledge assets. Yet most businesspeople have never been taught the fundamentals of knowledge as a business asset and as a value creation system. Part I will introduce you to knowledge as a fuel and as a raw material. It will re-introduce you to your own organization as a knowledge factory that creates value for your customers and drives the performance of your company. It will answer the questions:

- How is knowledge both a fuel and a raw material?
- How do organizations get paid for what they know?
- Do product companies get paid for what they know?
- Why are some industries having a hard time getting paid for their knowledge products?
- How does knowledge work as a business asset?
- What are the categories of knowledge raw materials?
- How do these raw materials get combined in a knowledge factory?

Even though knowledge seems like an abstract concept, the basic knowledge components of your business are actually very easy to identify and model. Part I will help you create a model of your knowledge factory. This visualization will improve your thinking and your communication about your business with your stakeholders. We hope that you will never see your business in the same way ever again.

Knowledge Is the New Oil

Oil

It is hard to imagine the tangible economy without oil. It fuels our cars and trucks. It generates electricity to power our factories and homes. It serves as a raw material for products we use every day, from plastics to fabrics, fertilizers, and high-tech materials. These many uses for oil have made this commodity a source of great wealth.

Like oil, knowledge is both a product and a raw material. It is an abundant asset that is a part, directly or indirectly, of everything we use. And it can make you very rich. Knowledge has already made many people rich. Just ask Bill Gates and Paul Allen, the founders of Microsoft. Or ask Sergey Brin and Larry Page, the founders of Google. These are the modern-day wildcatters, striking it rich by finding a new oil field with an essentially infinite supply. These wildcatters are a great illustration of the fact that there is a role for both luck and smarts in the knowledge business, or any business for that matter. But the story goes much deeper than these few success stories.

Knowledge has already grown to become the fuel and the raw material for over half of the production of our economy today. This trend will only continue. This shift to a knowledge economy means that you are already in the knowledge business whether you know it or not. Yet, if you go into the average business, there is no inventory of knowledge, no accounting for the investment and return on the organization's knowledge work. You didn't learn how to make this shift in school. But you have certainly experienced it. If you are over 40, you probably remember your first computer. If you are over 20, you probably remember the rise of the Internet. But even if you are going to school right now, you are probably not learning all you will need to know about how to live and work in this new world fueled by technology and the Internet. And if you are working, you are definitely not working in an organization optimized for this new world. Change has come too quickly and the way that businesses organize themselves has not kept up with this change. But the future is already here and knowledge is already the critical fuel and raw material of our era.

So it is about time to learn some of the basic economic characteristics of knowledge. This is important because knowledge breaks many of the rules of traditional economics and business. This chapter will help you understand knowledge as an economic good. Your organization is already getting paid for its knowledge in one way or another. We will help you understand how this works and how you can get paid in new ways by leveraging the special economic characteristics of knowledge. One of the big differences between oil and knowledge is that oil is a physical and finite good. Although it has been very abundant and has created great wealth in our society, the supply of oil is finite. In contrast, knowledge is infinite. Selling or giving away knowledge does not diminish your supply of knowledge and, often, collaboration and sharing can increase your original knowledge. Learning the basic economics of knowledge will help you turbocharge your business.

KNOWLEDGE STARTS AS A COMMODITY

The first thing to understand about knowledge is that, like oil, it is almost like a commodity, widely used and widely available. You could almost describe it as a natural resource. This resource is widely available in any library and on the Internet, and is given away regularly on television and in public schools. There is no more graphic demonstration of this than the recent launching of the MITOpenCourseWare Web site by the Massachusetts Institute of Technology. MIT asserts on the OpenCourseWare (OCW) home page that "OCW is a Web-based publication of virtually all MIT course content." Similarly YouTube recently launched YouTubeEDU which aggregates lectures published by universities. It has never been easier to access knowledge in its raw form at little or no charge.

Yet individuals and businesses regularly profit from knowledge. As you saw in the Introduction, over half of the value of the economy in the United States is in knowledge-based intangibles. This means that commoditized knowledge is regularly and profitably turned into products that can be sold. The fact that MIT has published its courseware on the Internet does not mean that it stopped charging $35,000+ in tuition to its students. And, although there will surely be changes in the future in the way that a university creates and gets paid for value, it is hard to imagine a future where there will not be students willing to pay a large amount of money to attend MIT.Beyond getting access to the courseware, also be able to interact with professors and students, and at the end of their stay, receive a diploma with the MIT brand on it.

The trick to getting paid for your knowledge is to package it in a form that connects with a market need. A lot of this book is about how to do that. And it is very necessary because the shift to a knowledge economy is causing huge disruption. The economics and opportunities of technology and knowledge are fueling change in almost every business. We take it for granted but computers have radically changed almost every business. We had a recent reminder when we took one of our cars to have a dent repaired. Walking through the auto body repair shop and into the owner's office, we were not surprised to see a computer on his desk. But then he started showing off his estimating software. It had information loaded about every make and model of car in the market. He explained that he could produce an estimate in a few minutes that would have taken hours in the "old days" when he would have had to search reference books and make phone calls to find the pricing of specific parts on a car. This has made his small business much more productive than in the past and created new value for the owner and for his customers. It has also changed the skill set needed to be successful in his business. All his competitors have the same software. So in order to compete, he has to be good at using the systems as well as making the actual auto body repairs. Even this small business has a knowledge factory.

The shift to a knowledge economy, however, is doing more than creating efficiencies. Technology and the Internet are also fueling huge disruptions in many businesses. A great example is the media business. Today newspapers, magazines, music companies, and even movie studios are struggling to maintain profitable businesses in the face of on-line competition. At the same time, technology businesses like IBM have shifted from being hardware suppliers to selling consulting and solutions. The lines between types of businesses are blurring more every day.

THE ECONOMICS OF KNOWLEDGE

As we move forward, you will begin to appreciate that knowledge is a fundamentally different kind of economic asset. Knowledge is infinite. Yes, you heard us correctly. Knowledge is an infinite asset. Giving it away or selling it does not diminish your supply of knowledge. This infinite nature of knowledge conflicts with one of the most basic assumptions of the economics that most of us learned in school: the concept of scarcity which says, "If you have 100 shirts and sell one, your inventory decreases." Knowledge assets do not follow this basic principle.

Take software for example. If your company writes a knowledge product like a piece of software, you can sell that software an infinite number of times without running out of software. If you deliver the software via a disk, you may run out of disks but that does not mean you ran out of software. The value of your software is not diminished just because you sell it to a lot of people. In fact, your software will probably improve over time because you can make revisions based on the experiences of your users. That means that the more users, the greater the potential for the software to actually improve over time.

Economist Paul Romer is one of the first proponents of New Growth Theory that tries to address the fundamental challenges to traditional economics that have arisen in the knowledge economy. He explains that if you have a scarce, physical resource, pricing will be driven up by that scarcity. The value of knowledge is different. It is more about utility. Romer says that the value of a knowledge asset "is proportional to the size of the market in which you can sell it."[1]

This is a really important concept. If you master it, this is the idea that will separate you from all other companies in your field. It is the challenge for which your company will be striving from this day forward. What Romer is telling us is that knowledge (not just software) does not become an economic good until it solves a problem in a way that people are willing to pay for the solution. Once you identify a solution, then the only limit to the value of that knowledge is how many people need the solution. Put another way, there are no physical constraints to the value of knowledge; the only limit is demand.

> *Knowledge does not become an economic good until it solves a problem . . . then the only limit to its value is how many people need the solution.*

It sounds obvious and not that different than physical goods. People only buy something they need or want. But you can run out of physical goods. You don't run out of knowledge. Plus, there's the fact that knowledge is a very malleable product. It can be shaped into so many forms that there are many more possibilities for getting paid. And it's more scalable. As long as you can continue to provide value, there are no limits to scaling your business based on the economics of knowledge. Interested? Let's dig in and look at how to get paid for your knowledge.

GETTING PAID DIRECTLY FOR KNOWLEDGE

Your company already has extensive knowledge. The question is how to package this knowledge in a tangible form that has economic value. To understand your business as a knowledge business, the best place to start is with your revenue line. What does it say there? What do the bills to your customers or clients say? Are you selling them a knowledge product, a physical product, a service, or the time of your employees?

Selling Knowledge Products

The first way of getting paid for what you know is to get paid directly through knowledge products. The simplest form of this kind of product is a written or spoken recording of knowledge. This includes books, articles, reports, and white papers—all of which can be delivered in physical or electronic form. Speaking can be delivered directly as a one-time experience or recorded as a reusable product. Video is becoming an increasingly common delivery form for knowledge products. Many informational products are also bundled: providing a book, workbook, and CD in one package.

In these forms, knowledge is very much a commodity. The competition for it is often free content. The amount of free content is increasing every day thanks to the Internet. So to get paid for knowledge, your product needs to provide some kind of synthesis of a body of knowledge. Sometimes the knowledge is unique. Most of the time, the synthesis and the approach are the unique aspect. Take this book for example. Much of what we are writing here is known. We didn't identify the shift to the knowledge economy. But we have experienced together with our clients the implications of that shift to the challenges of running a business today. And we have come up with a series of steps that help companies "see" and manage this side of their business in a way that helps them grow and improve performance. Our contribution is to tie it all together and package the knowledge in a way that businesspeople can apply it to improve their own operations.

The same knowledge in this book can (and will) be delivered in different forms. Before taking on the project of this book, Mary took a course from Dianna Booher. Dianna has written 44 books in total in her two areas of interest: Christianity and business communications. A couple of years ago, Mary heard Dianna speak and was convinced to take her class when she heard Dianna explain the two dozen product offshoots she had sold for a single book including foreign language editions, electronic editions, workbooks, training manuals, laminated "tips" sheets sold at office supply stores, and recordings of programs, to name a few. Of course, that does not count the number of speeches and training sessions based on the book where she and her employees delivered a "live" version of the content.

People like Dianna make a very good living selling synthesized knowledge. But selling a book is far from a guarantee of income. Each year in the United States, over 150,000 new books are published by major U.S. publishers. Many more are published privately through on-demand vendors. Yet, the average book will sell just 500 copies.[2] Most of them will not make a profit. These kinds of figures make it tough on authors who want to make a living from their writing. It is not too different from the star system that dominates in the music business, although the Internet may change these dynamics over time. Of course, many people write books as an adjunct to another business. Consultants write books to make their expertise tangible. Academics write books because publishing supports their career development. As you will see in later chapters, it is pretty common for businesses to give away knowledge products on the one hand to support their overall value and revenue creation model.

Licensing and Secondary Sales
Another way of getting paid for knowledge is through licensing. This usually applies to situations where there is a very clear technology or knowledge product that has specific legal protection. We will discuss intellectual property (IP) in more detail in the next chapter. The important thing to

understand at this point is that if your process, service, or product qualifies for legal protection, then you have a whole new way of monetizing your knowledge, through direct sale, licensing, and royalty streams.

One of Mary's recent guests on the monthly call for the Intangible Asset Finance Society (IAFS), David Ruder, shared the story of Massimo, a brand that was licensed to Target and has become a huge source of licensing revenue to its owners. Massimo was a lackluster branded apparel company until they licensed their name to Target in 2000, which now generates $1 billion in annual revenue with the brand.[3] Trademarks do not have an expiration. As such, they can be a great investment. In contrast, patents do have a limited life. But they can give a technological advantage to their owner. Because so many companies have patents which they have not exploited themselves, there is a growing secondary market in them. Another guest on the IAFS calls, David Hetzel, estimated that these kinds of sales yield $1 billion to $2 billion per year.[4]

Licensing or outright sale of IP can be powerful because it enables you to get paid in a new way for work you have already done. But, ultimately, you are still selling a "do it yourself" solution. The licensee/buyers, like the buyers of other kinds of knowledge products, have to contribute their own effort and expense to solving their problem; they must build a business around the IP. This characteristic puts knowledge products on the low end of the value spectrum from your customer's perspective. The knowledge product provides information, ideas, and suggestions on how to apply them. But it does not solve your customers' problems. For that, you need to sell them a service.

Getting Paid for Knowledge Services

It is common to hear our current economy referred to as a "service economy." This is because the rise of the knowledge economy means that more and more value is packaged for customers in the form of services. Service companies include anyone doing work for you outside of your own organization. Another word for service companies is outsourcers. Most people tend to think of outsourcing in the context of outsourced manufacturing because of the increased use of production facilities in countries like China and India.

But we would invite you to define outsourcing more broadly. You are outsourcing when you hire other companies to perform tasks as diverse as providing you electricity, manufacturing products you are going to sell, cleaning your office, handling your payroll, and solving your management problems. In each case, you are hiring someone for their expertise or focus. Outsourcing partners usually have a competency or process that you do not have and choose not to develop. But, in most cases, your outsourcing partners perform tasks that are critical to your operations.

Did you notice that we mentioned electrical power as outsourcing? At the beginning of the industrial era, factories were built next to rivers so that the water in the river could be harnessed to power the machines. Power generation had to be a core competency of any manufacturing organization. Over time, the rise of gas- and coal-powered generation facilities meant that electricity could be generated more efficiently by specialty companies so manufacturing companies could focus on what we see today as their core competency of making things. Electrical utilities were an early form of outsourcing.[5] (Of course, many believe that this trend will be reversed once again as companies exploit new technologies to produce their own power using sources such as wind and solar and creating microgrids, a completely new model.)

If we were to take this argument to its logical conclusion, we could make the case that all your suppliers and vendors are outsourcing partners. This is theoretically true but not necessarily very practical. You can buy many services and products on an arms-length basis. However, as you will learn later in this part and throughout this book, for your key external partners, there is a greater and greater need to manage the relationship and monitor their operations—because their mistakes become yours.

If you sell services, it is quite likely that your organization is itself an outsourcing partner to your customers. They are paying you for your expertise as well as for getting a job done. There are basically four ways to get paid for services.

Getting Paid for Services

1. Selling tasks
2. Selling time
3. Selling value
4. Selling solutions

Selling Tasks

The first way to get paid for a service knowledge-based is by the task. This is how a bicycle delivery person gets paid—there is a fee for each package delivered. Your dry cleaner gets paid for each article of clothing. Doctors get paid by the procedure.

Now, many service businesses have been around for years. We fully expect people to argue this point with us. You probably buy our argument that doctors are knowledge workers. But what makes a delivery person a knowledge worker? You may think that you are paying him because you don't want to do it yourself. And that's true. But the good ones get repeat business because they know how to manage their time and use the fastest routes to zip around town.

What would you think if the delivery person worked for UPS or FedEx? The knowledge component of their businesses is even more obvious. Everyone in their delivery chain has scanners so that it is backed up by an automated system that tracks the progress of your shipment as it makes its way across the country or across the world. These automated processes are a key part of what you are buying when you purchase from these companies.

Same thing is true with dry cleaners. Twenty years ago, we took our cleaning to a store in our neighborhood that had a manual ticket system with an owner who washed the shirts himself and turned them around in three to four days. When he retired, we went down the block to a more typical company. All their tickets are automated so they can look up our order by last name and have the automated hanging system stop at our order. They can turn clothes around in one day and have a list of all the clothes that have been dropped off so we don't need to keep track of all the tickets. Their records also enable them to offer discounts to frequent customers as part of a loyalty program. We still are just getting clothes cleaned but the automation is part of the value-add of this vendor.

Selling Time

Some services do not break down into simple units like procedures, packages, or pieces of clothing. That's why many services are priced around the amount of time your employee spends performing the task. This is a common pricing mechanism in construction, home and office care, consulting, and professional services like those supplied by lawyers and accountants. In all these cases, the underlying unit of exchange is the employee's time. Sometimes, the practice is to charge for a variable amount of time during each engagement. However, it is also common to offer a fixed fee to provide the service that may be adjusted if the original assumptions about the job conditions or description change.

This category has an interesting mix—manual laborers with what would seem to be a low knowledge component and what appears to be the highest-value knowledge workers: lawyers, accountants, and consultants. With manual laborers, you are essentially charging your customers for time or expertise with a specific kind of physical task. The major knowledge opportunities in this kind of business are around the processes to plan, monitor, and bill—that is, to manage the movement of workers and the monitoring of their work.

Ironically, many professionals are not much different than any other hourly worker. In fact, the only thing that separates the business models of professionals getting paid by the hour from manual workers is the content and price of the service (sorry, but it's true). Lawyers, accountants, and many consultants rarely leverage their knowledge into repeatable processes, which, you will learn later in this book, are the holy grail of the knowledge economy because they offer huge opportunities for financial leverage. They cannot imagine that some of what goes on inside their heads could be standardized and even productized. They are happy because they make a good living being paid directly for "customized" knowledge provided to the customer's order.

Selling Value

More complex problems lend themselves to getting paid for the value of the solution. Some professionals use value-based fixed pricing to increase the return on their time. In this model, the starting point is the expected result of the project: what is the economic benefit of the solution? Then, a fixed price that is anywhere from 5 to 10 percent of the expected return is set as the fee. This works for small firms where the risk/reward balance of this approach can be managed.

Another way to get paid for value is to leverage knowledge into more scalable forms. This trend has already begun on lower-end problems. Standard contracts and even widgets to produce contracts based on a questionnaire are available on the Internet. Software has replaced a lot of the work of bookkeepers and enables many people to fill out their own income tax forms. More and more assessment tools are delivered via Internet portals. In India, the Aravind Eye Care System is able to treat millions of cataract patients each year at a low cost (the service is free to many) because they have standardized the processes associated with surgery and run their hospitals 24 hours a day.

Many highly compensated professionals—accountants, consultants, lawyers, and doctors among them—will insist that all their work is designed specifically for each individual client. This is true and will always be true—to an extent. The same technology that has been disrupting the low end of the accounting and legal fields will continue to push into their mainstream business. We also believe that there will be huge opportunities in the area of consulting. As you will see in Parts II and III, the dominant information and management paradigms used today were developed during the industrial era. The shift to a knowledge economy is invisible in accounting systems and in the priorities of many management teams. Many, many of these gaps are filled today on an ad hoc basis by consultants of many kinds. The highest-end firms, such as McKinsey, will probably keep their hold the longest on individualized solutions.

However, the real opportunity will lie in the creation of repeatable, auditable information systems that provide the same degree of information as a specialized study at a fraction of the cost. The work of the IC Rating Network is a case in point. The IC Rating tool we all use provides an audit of the full portfolio of knowledge intangibles in an organization. This kind of review, using a comprehensive but standardized process, provides a complete snapshot of a company worthy of a large custom consulting project at a fraction of the price.

In a way, the work of professionals is being industrialized in a pattern not that different from the industrialization of production in past centuries. Many "craftsmen" will be disrupted on the low end. But opportunities will continue to exist on the high end and for the creation of high-quality, scalable offerings.

Selling Solutions

The final way to get paid for services is the solution sale. Here, you get paid to just be there and to ensure that something does (or does not) happen. Examples are security systems, copy systems, and so-called "designer doctors" who collect a retainer for being on call to their patients. With a security system, for example, you are paying for some equipment in your building and electronic monitoring services that ensure follow-up to any risks that are detected. Today over 70 percent of Xerox's revenue comes from multi-year contracts for consulting, technical services, and financing.[6] They are selling their customers continuous, seamless internal printing capabilities. Do they sell equipment? You bet. But the equipment has almost become the "razor" in the business—the anchor of the relationship with the real revenue coming over time from service contracts providing the continuing "razor-blade" income.

The most scalable form of the service-based sale of knowledge is software. It is common today to think of software as a physical product, the recorded code. But software is really a service, an automated form of problem solving for its users. The traditional way of pricing software today focuses on selling the software "package." Under this model, improvements to the software are often sold as upgrades and new releases. The focus was on the software as a product. The model here is Microsoft, which has been able to charge for a new license each time its users have switched hardware and/or charge for each new generation of its product, through several generations of Windows including Vista and, now, Windows 7.

There is a new trend emerging in software that is shifting this focus and creating a new business model called "software as a service." This model was made famous by Salesforce.com but is becoming more common throughout the software industry. Here, the software usually resides on the Internet and emphasis is on providing a consistent service to a company. Service is sold by the month or year. Upgrades and fixes to the software happen in the background. Changes and improvements get rolled out to clients without any need to upgrade the software on the client computer. Over time, customers of this software model may end up paying as much as the license fee for packaged software. But the value proposition is different and the level of service should be higher over time.

A great example of using software as a way of operationalizing knowledge and making it scalable is a company called HubSpot based in the Boston area. This company has created a platform for what they call "in-bound" marketing—the creation of business leads through blogging and social media. This software automates a lot of the things that good bloggers do: search engine optimization, landing pages, tracking other bloggers in your space (so you can comment), content management, analytics, and lead management. Most bloggers just post and wait for something to happen. Effective bloggers cobble together a number of data sources and platforms (most of them free) to get juice out of their content. But this can be time-consuming and the information is spread across a number of platforms. HubSpot automates a lot of these processes and adds functions that help shape your blog posts for maximum visibility. They can charge for their product because they save bloggers time and increase the marketing yield of their work.

Even if you do not sell software, you need to think about the shift in the software industry. Because, going back to Paul Romer's argument, it is possible to see all knowledge products as software, that is, packaged knowledge that automates the solution to a problem. As mentioned above, solutions sales are the most scalable business models for direct knowledge sales.

GETTING PAID *INDIRECTLY* FOR KNOWLEDGE

For all the attention that we have paid to this point to direct sales of knowledge, many companies still get paid just for providing a physical product. No services. No knowledge product. But don't be fooled. These companies (or at least the ones that survive) get paid for their knowledge as well.

This is very obvious in an iPod, which is a highly innovative delivery system of an on-line music service. Apple broke ground in many ways when they created the iPod including:

- The physical design of the product itself
- The creation of an on-line delivery system for the music and content loaded on the product
- The licensing arrangements with key content providers to convince them to make their product available through Apple

But it is also true for a company like Wal-Mart, which is known for the low cost of its merchandise. This cost advantage reflects its innovative:

- Retail information technology
- Supply chain management
- New efforts in energy use and impact

Time will tell whether Wal-Mart's understanding of the business opportunity presented by energy/environmental sustainability will also broaden its perspective on community and employee stakeholder relations.

Even companies getting paid directly for knowledge products or services have a lot of their value embedded in their internal processes that are not even visible to the client. Think about the systems at UPS and FedEx. There are truck route planning systems, package tracking systems, air hub systems, and many others that support the underlying service which is moving the package from one point to another. Customers of these companies are buying the quality and consistency that these systems ensure.

The truth is that a huge amount of the value of knowledge in most organizations is not isolated and individually identifiable—it exists as a system. The systems provide efficiency, quality, process improvement, and innovation. We'll be showing you more about these systems in the coming chapters.

YOU CAN GET PAID MANY WAYS FOR THE SAME KNOWLEDGE

Finally, it is important to point out that the same knowledge can be sold in multiple forms. Remember Dianna Booher's books? She gets paid many times in many different ways for the same basic knowledge. This strategy is not just applicable to consultants and speakers. Any company that develops a competency can package it in different forms for different markets.

A number of years ago, Hewlett-Packard (HP) outsourced its printer repair business to UPS. The decision was based on the understanding that the hardest part of the repair business was not the repair itself. The process of making repairs was well-documented and not very complex. The hard part for HP was getting the logistics right—to move the printer to a repair center and back to the customer without losing their shirts. If package logistics were the hard part, then UPS was a logical partner. From the perspective of UPS, this business was just another way to get paid for pushing packages through their distribution network.

Many niche businesses are built by companies that are very good at something and rather than just providing their service to their customers, they begin to sell services to their former competitors as well. One example is ProCent, software built by a successful commercial flooring contractor for its own operation. Because flooring is a regional market, there was no competitive threat to the company selling its software to contractors in other parts of the country. The small number of flooring contractors of significant size limits the end-user market but it was a great side business for someone inside the market.

Another model is franchising. Franchises get started by successful sole operators who perfect their processes and systems (or in Romer's vocabulary "software") to the point that they can sell a ready-to-go business to another entrepreneur to set up on their own. Franchises can have multiple payment streams associated with them to pay for management systems, brands, consulting services, and training.

THE DILEMMA OF FREE

Up to this point, we have focused on getting paid for what you know. But, of course, there is another big story in the knowledge economy—one that is still being written. Basically, one of the challenging truths of the knowledge economy is that you will end up giving away a lot of your knowledge. Google's search business is the simplest but most dramatic example of this. Their search business yields $20+ billion in advertising revenues each year. But the core product, the search itself, is free. In Chapter 3, we will dissect this business model a little more. But the important point here is that Google gives away huge amounts of value every day and still has managed to become one of the leading companies of the knowledge era thus far.

Another great example is the Grateful Dead. Long before the Internet and downloadable music, the Dead built a business model that was very different from other rock bands. They made their money from concert tickets and merchandise like tee shirts. They allowed people in their audiences to tape their performances—a practice strictly prohibited by other bands, who made most of their money from selling records. Along the way, the band developed a group of rabid fans called Deadheads, some of whom followed them from city to city. This strong community pioneered, in many ways, the approach taken today of countless business-people using social media to create communities with and for their customers.

The open source movement is another example of the free versus paid dilemma. This approach is most common in the software market. Java and Linux are the two largest examples of software that is developed by a community and available to all at no charge. Yet there are plenty of vendors that make money selling hardware, services, and related software to support the free and open product.

The open source approach is also being taken by selected hardware companies. An example that we have found very intriguing is Arduino, a company in Italy that put the designs of its simple electronic gadget on the Web. You can use its designs and build as many of your own gadgets as you want. The only restriction essentially is that you cannot use the Arduino brand. Users have used the designs to create projects as varied as a Wii controller for a remote control car, a breathalyzer microphone, and a miniature pocket piano. The company benefits from the improvements to the base design shared by their community and gets much more attention than it would if it were just a small company selling electronic gadgets. And it still makes money from selling its own gadgets.

The free-versus-paid dynamic also creates a lot of conflict with traditional approaches to intellectual property. Our legal system affords protection to certain kinds of knowledge assets through patent, trademark, and copyright systems. The ease of sharing and the open communication of the knowledge economy have created many threats to this system. Some, like the Pirate Party in Europe, advocate the elimination of this kind of property right. It is too hard to predict today where it will all end up. But we can tell you two things with certainty: You should find ways to share some of your knowledge for free and you will still have plenty of ways of making money. To understand this dynamic and the forces behind the demand for all your knowledge, it is helpful to examine the question of why you get paid.

WHY DO YOU GET PAID?

As we have made clear, the starting point for understanding your organizational knowledge is to identify the ways that you get paid for your knowledge. However, the need to give away some of your knowledge means that focusing exclusively on how you get paid will miss some of the critical knowledge that distinguishes your organization. In most cases, your customer is "buying" the whole package whether they pay for it or not, just as Google's advertising is buying access to the users of the free service. So to understand Google's search business or your own, you have to understand more than just the knowledge for which they or you get paid.

To identify the full picture of your critical knowledge, it is helpful then to move beyond the concept of products and services and ask three questions.

What Are Your Core Competencies?

To understand why your customers do business with you, it is helpful to first look deeper inside the organization. Competencies are a good place to start. Competencies are families of knowledge that are shared and captured within your organization. They represent knowledge that helps you do what you do. Some competencies are common across all the players in an industry. Airlines, for example, need to have competencies in managing fleets of planes, reservations, and routing systems. But not all airlines share Southwest's competency at developing an empowered workforce focused on the customer—a factor that has helped Southwest compete on both price and service. You will see in the next chapter that all companies have a unique set of competencies that distinguish them.

What Is the Problem You Solve?

Next, you want to move outside your organization and shift to a (maybe the) critical perspective for any strategic business decision—that of your current and prospective customers. Seeing yourself in their eyes is an important reality check and keeps the exercise connected with your everyday business. We recommend doing this with a good cross-section of your team.

This is unique to each situation. You may provide a product or service that is a component of your customer's value creation process. They may be outsourcing a function that they used to perform themselves and think that the cost or the quality would be improved by using a firm more expert in that function. It may just be a question of focus or interest—they may not want to bother with creating an internal equivalent to the solution you provide.

Most of the time, companies answer this question too narrowly, defining the problem as the product or service they provide rather than looking at the problem from the customer's perspective. A classic example is railroads that thought they were in the railroad business rather than the transportation business. A great recent example we heard on the radio was the growing sales of milk shakes by fast-food restaurants. The reason wasn't because Americans suddenly developed a taste for milk shakes but, rather, that more and more people commuting in their cars were discovering milk shakes as a neat way to eat breakfast on the way to work. The problem from the customers' perspective wasn't finding the ideal milk shake, it was finding a breakfast that wouldn't spill on their work clothes in a moving car.

Why Do They Choose You?

Of course, the obvious next question is how well you solve the problem for your customer. This may address how you stack up against the competition but it also gets to the second set of questions about how you do what you do. This is more of an internal question. What makes your organization different? This speaks to specific areas of expertise that help you not only solve today's problems but continue to innovate new solutions to tomorrow's problems.

Sun's CEO, Jonathan Schwartz, told a story in an entry on his blog on March 11, 2009, about how he closed a deal with a client for a million dollar contract for support on free software. He teased the customer at the closing, reminding him that the software was free. But the customer was willing to pay because it meant that he could call Sun's people, including Schwartz, if there was a problem with his implementation. His problems cost much more than the million dollar price tag. Sun's knowledge was a great insurance policy.[7]

CONCLUSION

Ultimately there are two core questions about how you get paid for your knowledge. The first is: *What is the value you create for your customers?* The second is: *How do you get paid for creating this value?* This chapter has helped you get a high-level sense of that value creation process and the many ways that you can get paid for what you know. Remember that you can get paid at either end: by selling knowledge directly or by using your knowledge to create value for your customers. The next chapter will show you a lot more about how to make this value real, to break down your knowledge into understandable, actionable components—the raw materials of your knowledge factory.

EXERCISE

How do you get paid for your knowledge?

- What is the problem you solve?
- How do you get paid?
- What knowledge do you give away?
- Why do your customers choose you?

You can download a worksheet for this exercise at www.intangiblecapitalbook.com.

Intangibles Are the New Raw Materials

Raw Materials

In the tangible economy, raw materials are combined and sometimes trans-
formed to make finished goods. It is often impossible to see the different raw
materials in the finished product—together, they make something completely
new. In fact, there is often a progression of processes that leads to a final
product. Stalks of wheat, for example, are processed and ground to make flour
which then goes into making bread. Grains of sand become silicon in
computer chips and oil becomes a high-tech plastic.

The raw materials of the knowledge era are knowledge-based intangibles. You may be nodding your head as you read this. But do you
really know what it means? If not, you are not alone. Knowledge continues to be seen as an amorphous, misunderstood part of business. This
widespread ignorance isn't helped by the vocabulary. The word *intangibles*
itself is troubling because its very definition implies that an intangible is invisible, untouchable, and unknowable. The word *knowledge* is also very general and lacks a specific connotation for business value creation. Yet
knowledge is the core asset of this century.

We started this book talking about how to get paid for knowledge
because we wanted you to understand the central importance of knowledge
to your business. It is not a "nice to have" luxury of upscale companies.
Knowledge is a critical resource for every business from the most humble
service and product companies to the highest of the high tech. You can
probably think of a million examples of how your own workplace has
changed in the last 10 to 20 years thanks to computers. But you may not

have realized how the accumulated effect of all these changes has fundamentally altered your business.

What does this kind of computerization and the resulting growth of knowledge mean to your business? Answering that is the job of this chapter. Here, you will learn to distinguish between the four basic types of knowledge assets that become the raw material for your value creation: human, relationship, structural, and strategic capital. You will learn to think about their relationship to the two main functions of your business: value creation and support services. You will learn about the critical components of each type of asset. And you will also learn about the secret power of structural capital—the Holy Grail of the knowledge era.

None of these are new categories of assets. People, customers, production processes, and strategies have always been the building blocks of business. What has changed is that these knowledge intangibles have moved from a supporting to a starring role in business models. Even the future of manufacturing is dependent less on tangibles and more on intangibles such as a trained workforce, a culture that supports continuous improvement, a network that maximizes the quality and cost of your total production process, and structural knowledge that ensures consistency as well as serving as a launchpad for innovation. Buying equipment is not the hard part—getting all the intangibles right is.

THE TWO FAMILIES OF ORGANIZATIONAL ASSETS

As we move through this chapter and really the rest of the book, there is a distinction we want to make about the organization of businesses. It is inspired by the Value Chain graphic created by Michael Porter back in 1985, shown in Figure 2.1.[1] This simple graphic is a great illustration of the generic business model for the industrial era. Most of us still carry this vision around in our heads even though the average organization no longer looks like this. Porter's graphic reflects the fact that most organizations in the industrial era created a product, usually in a pretty linear fashion. This was the value creation process of the business. To facilitate the value creation side of its business, every organization also had (and still has) a series of support services. Porter's original set included firm infrastructure, human resource management, technology development, and procurement. We have modified these somewhat to focus on human resource management, information technology, finance, and accounting.

The simple linearity of the value creation process in Porter's graphic was in a way a representation of the production line in a factory. In this chapter and in Chapter 3, you will see a different vision of the value creation process that is more appropriate to the knowledge era. But we want to make the distinction between the two basic functions: value creation and support services. Most of this book is focused on the value creation process as the way that you get paid for your knowledge. However, many of the approaches and tools for intangibles management can also be applied to the

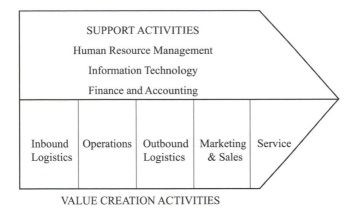

Based on Porter, *Competitive Advantage*

Figure 2.1 Value Chain.

various support services described above that are part of every business. We'll share some ideas on how to do this as we go along.

Some may question the classification of information technology (IT) as a support layer since it is so closely intertwined with the rise of the knowledge era. Yet, IT is relatively mature as a business function that supports the work of the company, its value creation process. That aspect of your IT function can and should be seen as a support service to the rest of the organization. Now, let's turn to the components of the knowledge side of your business.

HUMAN CAPITAL

Knowledge in an organization begins and ends with people. The knowledge and experience that employees bring to their work is probably the greatest driver of an organization's success. What employees know helps to build an organization as well as to preserve, maintain, and improve it. This importance is generally accepted. It is rare to meet a CEO who won't tell you that his or her organization has the "best people" in the market. But this kind of statement is rarely challenged. Most businesspeople still don't know how to see beyond the people and understand the employees and managers of an organization as knowledge assets—as human capital.

There are some that are critical of the label "human capital." To them, it seems to smack of an attitude that people are just nameless cogs in an organization, exploited for their knowledge and experience. We don't share that view. In fact, we like the term *human capital* because it is a graphic statement of the fact that people are indeed an asset of the organization. Assets require investment and maintenance. And they are a critical part of the productive capacity of the organization. To us, this is the realization that matters—that your people are part of your productive capacity, now more so than ever. Because the future of your company depends on what you know rather than what you own. And what you know as an organization is intimately tied to the knowledge and experience of the people in your organization. In looking at human capital, it is helpful to distinguish between employees and managers. Both groups are employees but managers need a set of competencies that is distinct from those required for your value creation processes.

> *The future of your company depends on what you know rather than what you own.*

Employees

Each human being is different. As employees, human beings bring unique talents and abilities to their employers. This diverse skill set brings a richness to an organization that can be difficult to capture. We will show you techniques to understand this diversity in Chapter 4 but for now, do not let this richness keep you from trying to understand your human capital as a productive asset. There are actually some very clear ways of describing employee groups:

Competencies

We ended the last chapter by discussing the reasons why your customers choose your organization above others. There can be many reasons for this—but almost all can be traced back to the core competencies of your organization. Competencies are a way of thinking about the knowledge behind your revenue streams and your value creation processes. Competencies are also one of the basic ways of understanding the knowledge contained in your human capital. When we work with companies, we try to get the management team to define the competencies needed at the corporate or group level. This kind of thinking can be pushed down to the level of each employee. The core competencies of an organization are related to its value creation processes. Please remember that there are also a separate set of competencies related to support services that are specific to the function such as accounting or information technology. These need to be understood but are apart from the core competencies associated with value creation that we examine here.

For example, project management is a core competency for a number of our client companies but this competency is matched by others that are unique to their specific businesses, to the kinds of projects they manage. One has deep knowledge of the FDA requirements for software development. Another has a pool of expertise that includes master craftsmen who can do challenging custom jobs better than anyone else in their market. A third delivers help desk solutions for IT users around the country.

Competencies help you identify what is important in your employees' work. They can be described pretty explicitly. They can be measured. They can be used as a basis for hiring and promotion. They are the right starting point for developing a clear picture of your employees as a productive asset, as part of your knowledge capital.

Experience

Another way of understanding the depth of knowledge represented by human capital is experience. Although the number of years of work is not, in itself, a guarantee of a high level of knowledge, it is generally a good starting indicator. Of course, not every company understands this. Circuit City famously dismissed all their experienced salespeople the year before they went bankrupt to lower their average personnel costs.

Mixing types and levels of experience is a common way of developing balanced teams within an organization. One of the big fears of the aging workforce is that the experience and knowledge of Baby Boomers will be irrevocably lost as they retire. Meeting this challenge will require improved intangibles management that takes the kind of broad view of organizational knowledge such as that described in this book.

Longevity and Turnover

Longevity and turnover are related to experience as a way of framing human capital. In fact, they used to be critical metrics of the strength of a workforce. In today's more mobile world where large amounts of an organization's work may be done outside the normal employee base, these factors are less important. An employee's choice to stay at a company is still a positive thing. But the dynamism of our economy has made it harder for companies and employees to stay in one place for their whole career. As such, an employee with decades of service to a single company is no longer the norm, nor a requirement for stability and growth.

Nevertheless, turnover can be an important factor in the formation of human capital. Examples of high-turnover jobs include bank tellers, caregivers, and call-center workers. In most organizations, these kinds of roles do not contribute to creation of a lot of new knowledge capital because of the short average staff tenure. In fact, companies lose knowledge and incur considerable costs to keep a constant stream of new employees coming into the organization. There is something of a chicken-and-egg situation with high-turnover jobs—which comes first: the tedium and pressure of the way the jobs are structured or the high turnover? Mitigating the tedium and empowering employees can be an antidote to the costs of high turnover.

Attitude

We all know without seeing research that a good attitude can make the difference between effective and ineffective employees. In case you have any doubt, we can cite research that compares the performance of the companies on *Fortune*'s list of the "100 Best Companies to Work for in America." A study by Alex Edmans showed that the performance of these companies from 1984 to 2005 exceeded that of the overall market by 4 percent.[2]

Management

Management is a separate category within human capital. Not because they are not employees. They are. And they can and should be described as part of the profiling of employees. But managers also have a separate set of competencies and roles that are required to complete their jobs.

This book is about the many ways in which the job of the manager is changing in the knowledge era. These changes are reflected throughout the book and addressed very specifically in Chapter 5 which describes the evolution from command and control as the management paradigm to one of orchestration, driven by the growing importance of knowledge in the workplace.

The strength of management can actually be examined using criteria similar to those outlined for employees above: competencies, experience, longevity and turnover, and attitude. Competencies and experience are related to the managerial role being played. Longevity and turnover can play an even more powerful role with a manager. Longevity can bring depth of organizational understanding but be a barrier to change. A manager's attitude can have an influence way beyond his or her own work and affect entire teams or the whole organization.

RELATIONSHIP CAPITAL

As with human capital, relationship capital has always been a part of business. Organizations have always had customers, vendors, and financing partners, to name a few. But the nature of these relationships has been changing more dramatically in recent years. First of all, networking technology has made it easier to outsource pieces of a business that were formerly inside the corporation. The relationships with critical outsourcing partners are closer than that of arms-length client-vendor relationships. You may find yourself on both sides of this dynamic, performing outsourced services for your customers as well as outsourcing some of your internal processes to a vendor. Technology also facilitates customization and co-creation, which has made it easier for customers to play the role of innovation partners with your organization, again more intimate than a classic customer relationship.

Nowhere is this growing importance of relationships more obvious than on the Internet. In the next chapter, you will read how Google's search business is so clearly and intimately tied to its users and its advertisers. These shifts help us understand relationships as a two-way knowledge asset. The lines between customers, suppliers, users, and relationships of all kinds are starting to blur. Every company has a unique set of knowledge assets and this uniqueness extends to its combination of relationships.

So if you want to understand the nature and strength of a company's knowledge assets, you must understand the nature and strength of their relationship capital. Where to look? We will lay out three basic categories of relationship capital: customers, partners, and brands.

Customers

Where is the knowledge in customer relationships? It is in the shared understanding of each others' businesses. You know an enormous amount about your best customers: their history, their culture, their product or service requirements, their current market position, and their goals for the future. You can probably name their management team and a large number of their staff. People in your organization have personal relationships with many of the people in their organization enabling any of you to pick up the phone and talk about challenges and opportunities you see. Sometimes you will even know about the personal life of your counterpart. You will know and care about each other as individuals.

In today's world, it is increasingly common for companies to share information electronically and even be directly networked together. This kind of link serves to strengthen your relationship but also to make it harder to end it. And the existence of an electronic network means that you are sharing information in real time. All this is knowledge. And all this knowledge gives you strength and power.

Partners

Relationships with other kinds of partners are growing stronger and more important for the same reasons as those described for customers: increased outsourcing, increased linking of systems, and the need for co-creation and innovation. We will talk about partnerships in value creation and those that provide support systems for your organization.

Value creation partnerships are those related to your core business—the things you do to get paid and what you do to solve your customers' problems. Traditional suppliers for a manufacturer would fall into this category as they provide an input to the ultimate product sold to the manufacturer's customers. A service company that uses contractors for some of its workforce or for specific projects is using relationship capital as a substitute for its own human capital. You can see that the lines between the types of knowledge capital are blurry, which is why we devote the next chapter to the concept of understanding how knowledge assets work together as a system.

Your organization develops a deep knowledge of your vendors' businesses, their strengths and weaknesses, and how you can best work together. Technology makes it easier than ever for you to connect and collaborate with your vendors. A great illustration of this potential is the Boeing 787. The design of this plane represented a new approach by Boeing. Using an electronic system, the company was on-line with the hundred or so key vendors that would manufacture components and parts for the jet. More than ever before, Boeing pushed the design decisions out to the vendors, each of whom has specific expertise related to their part of the plane. The specifications that Boeing supplied were dramatically reduced from past plane projects reflecting the fact that Boeing gave each supplier greater freedom to innovate and design in their specific arena. But because the suppliers were all on-line together, the designs could be coordinated and integrated into the overall design. This approach reflected an increasing faith by Boeing in its relationship capital with its suppliers. It also reflected a change in Boeing's view of its core competency away from design to design coordination, assembly, and marketing of planes.

If you are familiar with this story, you may be surprised that we included it. Because the process has not gone smoothly and, as of the printing of this book, delivery of the plane was expected to be in 2010, two to three years after the original target. But no matter what happens, this experience will provide incredible lessons about how to manufacture in the knowledge era. Boeing is learning these lessons long before many others in the market. It is a case worth following so that you can learn from it too.

Your organization probably also has a number of partners related to your support services. Some services such as accounting, legal, and media have a long history of outsourcing. But better communication and technology are leading companies to also outsource more functions in the areas of finance, payroll, IT, and administrative services. Ideally, the decision to outsource a process reflects a realization that the competencies and systems needed to deliver that process are not core for your organization—but are core for your partner. That means that they will be able to do the work more efficiently and effectively than your own organization. Although price is always part of the consideration, price should not be the only point of evaluation as we will explain in the section below on intangibles management. If you pick a smart outsourcing partner, this relationship capital becomes part of your knowledge capital. But that means that you will also need to manage the relationship closely, in the same way and with the same care as internal processes.

Some of the most dramatic crises come when a company's partner fails to live up to expectations—both in value creation and support processes. In the past, Nike had problems related to child labor used in suppliers' factories. Mattel has had issues with lead paint used by their outsourced manufacturers. Kellogg has had to deal with *Salmonella* in peanut butter used to make crackers. These cases illustrate that relationships carry significant risk for the organization. In Chapter 8 we will talk about the fact that the intangible "balance sheet" includes both assets and liabilities associated with all intangibles like relationships. Relationships reach outside the traditional boundaries of an organization. But they should almost always be viewed as an integral part of the business's value creation "factory."

In the last chapter of this book, we will introduce other stakeholders who, although they do not play a direct role in value creation, are very important to the organization. These include investors, regulators, politicians, and the community at large.

Brands and Reputation

The final category of relationship capital is brand and reputation capital. Brand is how your customers see your products. Reputation is about how all your stakeholders view your entire operation. Each is important. Brand communication is generally thought to leave more room for definition by the holder. That is, I can influence how you see my brand through my marketing and management of the customer experience. But really both brand and reputation are as much about your stakeholders' knowledge of you as it is your knowledge of them. This shared knowledge is what make brand and reputation part of relationship capital.

In this point of view, brand and reputation are assets of the modern organization. The value of these assets is determined by your stakeholders. In the final chapter of this book we make the case that reputation is becoming as important as net income as the "bottom line" of your business. Net income tells you whether you made a profit last year. Reputation tells you whether your stakeholders have confidence in your ability to deliver a profit in the coming year.

It's no secret that the management of brand and reputation are changing in the Internet-enabled world where information is more available than ever. Word can spread like wildfire via the Internet and social media that include Twitter and Facebook about mistakes and missteps an organization makes. The way people spend their time is changing how they receive and process information about the products they buy. Like so many other aspects of management, the dominant way of managing brand and reputation in the past was from the top down—controlling the message that is delivered to customers and stakeholders.

However, these models are breaking apart. Advertising in mass media is being replaced with customer experience in on-line communities. Internet-enabled word of mouth can create viral marketing opportunities that could never be bought. It is no longer about what you say about your organization but, rather, about letting your actions speak for you. As our mothers told us, "actions speak louder than words." This new paradigm of branding has the potential to create stronger and more genuine relationships than a television commercial ever could.

STRUCTURAL CAPITAL

If you understand human and relationship capital, you can start a business. If your business creates value for your customers, you can earn a good living. But you will never grow large or particularly rich with just these two kinds of knowledge assets. This is because the real promise of the knowledge economy comes in the creation of structural capital, that is, knowledge that gets captured and institutionalized in an organization.

When people say that "all our assets walk out the door at night" they are showing their ignorance of structural capital. A really successful business has standardized processes and shared knowledge that stay in the company when people go home at night. Some, but far from all, structural knowledge can be protected legally and will become intellectual property. But, at this point, that distinction isn't important. First you want to understand how structural capital is formed and managed.

When people say that "all our assets walk out the door at night" they are showing their ignorance of structural capital.

Before we move forward, let us admit that structural capital, like so many of the terms used in intangibles management, has a branding problem. We can't tell you how many consultants and businesspeople have told us, "We can't use that phrase in front of our clients/managers," fearing that they would draw blank stares. We use the phrase because it's the phrase used in the literature and it is actually a nice description of what it is: knowledge that has been captured and becomes part of the organization. It is the infrastructure of the knowledge factory that we will describe to you in the next chapter.

In our experience, businesspeople have no problem with the term when it is used to explain the potential within their organization. We recently had this kind of experience with a management team. We had been hired to help them think about how to scale their organization. They already had offices all across the country but they had only tapped a small portion of their potential market. We came up with a summary that showed that they had strong competencies and strong relationships. But the structural capital was weak. The general manager got it immediately and asked us to do a structural capital gap analysis. Not only did he understand the concept, he packaged it for us as a new offering for our firm!

Once you understand the concept of structural capital, we think that you will embrace it, too. Having said all that, our advice is to use a name that resonates with your individual organization. Choose one that works: structural knowledge, organizational knowledge, knowledge infrastructure, organizational capital, or anything else that works. The important thing is to get beyond the name and get people in your organization to focus on the concept.

Because the truth is that structural capital is the Holy Grail of knowledge economy. It is the way that your organization captures knowledge and makes it re-usable. Remember what we said in Chapter 1 about how knowledge is an infinite asset? It is through structural capital that you can realize this promise and make your business scalable.

For purposes of this book and of your own understanding of your business, we will discuss four basic forms of structural capital: culture, organizational knowledge, intellectual property (IP), and processes. Please know that there is a lot of overlap between these forms. Organizational knowledge, for example, can be converted to process and may even be protected as IP. We make the distinction mainly to discuss specific characteristics of the individual forms even though all structural capital is, at its roots, captured knowledge of one form or another.

Culture

Culture is the least tangible of the structural capital assets. It can be hard to define but everyone knows it is there. Culture can be a productive or a destructive force within an organization. In general, a culture is what it is—and can be especially hard to change. As a starting point, it is important to be able to describe the basic features of a culture as a first step to self-knowledge.

In the IC Rating process that we use to map out the intangibles of organizations, culture characteristics are captured although they do not feed into the overall rating of the intangibles. The logic is that there is no one right culture but that understanding the predominant culture is critical to the success of all other management efforts. That's pretty much the way we view it, although we know that there are people who specialize in trying to change culture. And we know from experience that a bad fit between management efforts and existing culture can be a recipe for failure.

We recently had an experience with a very numbers-based organization. Their corporate culture demands precise calculations of everything. We had been hired to help them grow their organization. As a way of setting the stage for the project, we put up a drawing that showed the huge gap between the market coverage of their existing staff and the potential market—on the order of 50:1. Yet when they saw this graphic, the management team ignored this amazing disparity between their existing and potential markets. Instead, they immediately started arguing about the accuracy of the numbers behind the ratio (that would, by the way, have changed the 50:1 ratio only slightly). From that experience, we learned to vet every number so that this kind of discussion wouldn't derail our future conversations—although we have never let up in trying to help the team see the forest for the trees.

A good place to start in understanding your own culture is to use the following basic dimensions of culture including:

- The extent to which the business culture is homogeneous or heterogeneous
- The extent to which there are counteracting subcultures
- The extent to which it is difficult to adapt to the culture
- The extent to which the vision, mission, and goals of the organization are communicated and understood throughout the organization
- The extent to which the employees consider the working environment open
- The extent to which employees have a sense of pride in their workplace

When you are ready to dig deeper, you will want to provoke a discussion among staff members and management. The focus should be on the values and behaviors that the culture encourages. Self-understanding is the first step in understanding culture.

Organizational Knowledge

Organizational knowledge is a more explicit form of structural capital. This is all the knowledge that is captured and recorded in your company. This means that every product design, every process map, every training manual, every formula, every document, every e-mail, every entry ever made in a knowledge management system is part of your organizational knowledge. It includes all the knowledge that is being captured from your human and relationship capital. And capturing it is an important first step to the process of leveraging it.

Another way to think about organizational knowledge is as your own knowledge products. Some of these products, such as white papers, may actually be created for external purposes. But the great majority of these knowledge products are created to support your internal operations for either value creation or support services. And it all melds together to form a package that is your company's way of doing things.

We learned this lesson years ago, during the start-up phase of a project with a new client. As we spent time with staffers at all levels in this consulting and engineering company, we kept hearing a phrase over and over, "the way we do things." We finally coined the term the "Intertech Way" as a catchall for this concept: the processes, the approach, the attitude, the know-how, and the systems that this company applies in everything they do. Over time, we helped the company make the Intertech Way more tangible and visible for staff as well as for clients. One of the offshoots was a giant process map that they put on the wall and used to explain their value-add to clients. After spending a couple of hours talking through the process map, one prospect said, "I now understand that you know much more about this than we do and that will make you a good partner for us."

Intellectual Property

Intellectual property is a term that is usually used to refer to specific types of structural knowledge that enjoy special legal status. These include patents, trademarks, copyrights, and trade secrets. Each of these categories has a specific body of law associated with it. Patents have to be approved by a national authority. Other categories do not require registration but are still protected under the law.

Legal protection can create a significant competitive advantage, depending on the circumstances. As you saw in the previous chapter, this legal definition and protection can also create opportunities for licensing IP rights outside the corporation. This strategy is getting a lot more attention today from organizations, consultants, and software companies.

However, legal protection processes can be expensive and legal protection in itself is not a guarantee of competitive advantage. So, while you want to consult a good attorney to get the intricacies of the law correct, you should also try to seek the advice of someone that has a good grasp of the strategic role of IP. You want to make sure that you file for protection when it makes sense. This decision involves a cost-benefit analysis. Some of the factors to consider include the cost of filing, the risk of disclosing your invention (disclosure is the only way to identify the idea that you want to protect), the competitive benefit of having a protected idea, and the monetary benefit of being able to enforce and/or license your rights to others. Once you win a right, there are the practical and logistical challenges of managing the rights you obtain.

But these special legal systems are not the only way to "protect" your intangible capital. Jackie Hutter, a self-described "recovering patent attorney," pointed out to us that contracts are actually one of the most important ways of protecting your intangible capital. Good management of contractual relationships can have a big influence in customer and partner relationships (relationship capital) as well as key employee relationships (human capital) and acquired knowledge (structural capital).

One of the main ways that intangible capital gets protected is through its association with a strong business model. This goes for IP as much as for other kinds of intangibles. In the next chapter, you will see that the power of each of the components of your intangible capital is increased when they are combined with other knowledge components. Intangibles are a great example of the saying that "the value of the whole is greater than the sum of the parts." Although someone could steal or imitate specific aspects of your business, it is hard to duplicate the whole system. This is a major way that most companies attain and retain competitive advantage—and protect their IP. This is important to keep in mind because many in the IP community will try to tell you that the only intangibles of any value are IP assets. We strongly disagree, which is why we have taken so much time to explain all the elements of intangible capital.

We actually created a pretty big controversy with an earlier draft of this chapter. When we started out, we intended to define all structural knowledge as intellectual property. When we consulted colleagues in the business and legal communities on the draft, we got some strong support and some equally strong pushback. The conversation spilled over to Twitter and Mary's blog which had a record number of comments on a post called, "What's the right definition of intellectual property?" The message that we wanted to communicate is that all intangibles are important and legal protection is just one of the strategies to protect your intangibles. However, it became clear to us that insistence on this definition was going to distract a lot of people from the core messages of this book. So we backed down.

So our advice is to leave the term intellectual property to the lawyers. But do not leave the protection of your intangible capital to just a legal strategy. Come to understand it and protect it as a system. And remember the lessons of the last chapter. The highest value knowledge is knowledge that has been operationalized, put to work. The way that this usually occurs is actually through the creation of processes.

Process Capital

Process is not new to business. In fact, process in the form of production lines was a critical driver of the growth of the industrial economy. In a factory, you could see the physical movement of raw material as it flowed from the warehouse into a series of production lines with finished goods coming out the other end. The movement of goods, the productivity of the machines, and the output of the entire factory could be tracked. Accounting and operational systems made it possible to measure everything from the purchase of the land to build the factory down to the last widget being put onto a truck. It also, by the way, made it easier for bosses to identify the best way to do a task and mandate the work patterns of their workers. So much of what is accepted as "best practices" in management comes from the factories of the industrial era.

But today, a lot of process occurs inside of people's heads, their computers, and networks of computers spread across a building or across the globe. This kind of process can be harder to see and measure. The information gap begins from the initial investment, which is generally not tracked, all the way through to the end result. This lack of information keeps processes off the radar of many critical stakeholders from Boards of Directors to investors and sometimes even a management team. Many knowledge processes, therefore, are done on an ad hoc basis with people reinventing the wheel every day, day after day, year after year.

We have experienced this gap in companies of all sizes. In one middle market commercial specialty contracting company, we found that every one of their staff members had to be an expert with extensive industry experience because there was no process supporting them. This kind of contractor knows a certain piece of the building trade such as electrical, plumbing, or flooring. Success in this business requires excellence in estimating the job, buying the materials, and supervising the labor. This company had grown to be one of the largest in the United States by hiring very experienced people. But many of the details of the business were in the heads of their people. The bigger they got, the harder it got for individuals to remember everything. Each developed their rules of thumb for calculations and their own tracking systems. But each person's rules of thumb were different. Further, no one had access to good information. This led to all kinds of mistakes and misunderstandings—and a volatile work environment. The company only brought us in as consultants when key people started to leave in frustration. It was a slow and painful process to get people to use common systems and institutionalize their collective knowledge. Key new processes were implemented. As with any company there are plenty more horizons for continuous improvement but they are now past the chaos that forced them to begin to institutionalize their processes.

We have also seen this problem in larger companies where many of their processes are well-defined and institutionalized, there are often dramatic pockets where people do much of their work in their own way. One recent client had 70 people spread all across the country with only limited structural capital at their disposal—a Customer Relationship Management (CRM) system and some marketing materials. In conversations with these people, it was clear they were looking for more "support" in the form of content and processes. Interestingly, their managers were hesitant to standardize work processes—they didn't want to force everyone into a cookie-cutter approach. This is another good illustration of the top-down/bottom-up challenge facing managers of all kinds in the knowledge era. In this case, both management and employees came to see the value of creating shared content such as training materials and information systems that helped the field staff do their work more efficiently—while still leaving plenty of room for individual creativity and initiative.

It is important to note that knowledge processes and physical production processes are intersecting with greater frequency. This is because many of the marginal gains from manufacturing are now coming through automation of information or through adjustments to a process designed by employees who work on it. We have seen this in plant tours over the years. When we walk around a manufacturing plant today, most of the conversation is about how the workers organize their work teams and the flow of information. It is about the processes much more than it's about the machines.

Another factor coming into play is the increasing rate of outsourcing. The more critical an outsourced process is to the operation of a company, the greater the need for deep understanding of the underlying process. The best kind of outsourcing is where the process and knowledge of the outsourcing company is combined with special knowledge of the company to which the process is outsourced. In the HP–UPS example cited in the last chapter, HP's understanding of printer repair was supplemented by UPS's logistical expertise.

It is important to remember that automated processes are the most scalable forms of knowledge capital. Any time that you capture the "best practices" of your organization in an automated process, you are making every employee smarter when they come to work in the morning. They do not have to think about how to solve the simple problems—because the solution is already built into the system. For example, in the specialty contracting business, standardized systems for pricing, product yields, and preset assemblies of materials automate the estimating process. This frees the staff to think about the aspects of a project that are not standard—and how to protect the company in the structure of the bid. Then, the real opportunity comes when the information from the estimating system can be compared in real time to the actual results so there is a continuing loop of learning and improvement. Through continuous use and adaptation of systems like this, organizations can capture the wisdom and knowledge of each employee. These systems make everyone smarter and more effective. Good systems also make it possible for people to back each other up.

So, what are the key processes in your organization? Let's look at two basic categories of processes: those that support value creation for customers and those that support the internal operations of the company. Each company has its own set of value creation processes. They may include a combination of physical and computerized processes. In the contracting example above, the three key processes are estimating, purchasing, and project management. The easiest way to identify the key value processes in your organization is to start with how you get paid and work backward. What do you have to do to create and deliver value that solves your customers' problems? As you look at this question, you may realize that your process is ad hoc and not formal at all. But it still should be considered a process. And you should subject it to all the kinds of modeling and analysis suggested in this book. The less formal it is today, the more opportunity there may be for automating it in the future.

Of course, every company must also have a series of support processes. This list is much more standard and includes infrastructure, human resources, information technology, and finance. Each of these functions has its own body of knowledge, competencies, and processes. Although they are part of the intangible capital of your organization, we won't spend a lot of time on the details of these classic support systems because these functions are pretty mature.

However, there are two new processes that will be added to the standard set listed above: innovation and knowledge management. Chapter 6 goes into more detail about innovation but we will deal with knowledge management here.

Knowledge Management: A New Core Process

Knowledge management (KM) was actually one of the earliest solutions offered by the market in response to the rise of the knowledge economy. The message was simple: If we live in a knowledge economy, we need to manage knowledge. Software and consulting companies sold a lot of people on the concept of KM driven by a faith that if people in an organization could just have access to all the knowledge of their peers, everyone would be smarter and more effective. As often happens with new trends (which always walk the line of fads . . .) a lot of people thought that this single business function would provide *the* answer to management in the knowledge era. Check the box and you are a modern company. Of course, this faith was misplaced. This book is a testament to the fact that knowledge and the management of knowledge is about more than a software program.

But that does not mean that KM is irrelevant. It is actually an important tool and/or tactic that has relevance to almost every organization. The field of knowledge management continues to make contributions to the art and science of making vast amounts of information available to users. There will continue to be a need for experts who know how to create, organize, and access the right data points from pools of knowledge. This aspect of KM will continue to be a discrete competency and should be operationalized into knowledge management processes within every organization.

Having said that, there are a few other points that we should make. First, there are those who think that knowledge management will eventually be absorbed into all the other parts of the organization. This is an interesting argument. To us, it says that knowledge management will become a core competency of all knowledge workers. And that is true. All knowledge workers will have to develop a greater understanding of and take greater responsibility for the management of information and knowledge that they need in their work. Nevertheless, their organizations will have responsibility for building the systems and/or providing access to media that will facilitate their personal knowledge management.

Second, there are some who see social media as a replacement for KM. We think that, indeed, social media can and should replace some forms of knowledge management. In this view, social media can be seen as a tool for real-time knowledge access—when you have a question, you just put it out to the right network and chances are, you will get what you need.

This is yet another example of the top versus bottom dynamic in the knowledge-era enterprise. The initial approach of knowledge management was a top-down initiative, creating the structure and then requesting (or mandating) participation. A great example of this is the management consulting firm McKinsey. Michael had a young colleague who worked at McKinsey after receiving his MBA in the early parts of the 2000s. He reported that a critical part of his job as a junior consultant was writing up information about projects so that it was available for everyone else in the firm. The motivating factor is for the junior person to get visibility for his or her work by those higher up in the organization. There is no doubt that this kind of system is created for and run from the top down. There continue to be systems run in this way.

However, there are many more examples about knowledge from the bottom up. Some of the most striking stories come from the military, an organization traditionally associated with top-down command and control. The Army recently put a number of its field manuals on wikis open to anyone with access to the Army Internet system. This means that soldiers and officers from all levels can suggest changes to the manuals. The thought is that the best people to create manuals are those with experience on the ground.[3]

During the Iraq War, a number of dedicated social media sites have been created for soldiers. An example is companycommand.army.mil, a site for Company Commanders in the Army. This and similar sites provide a place for active soldiers and their leaders to share ideas, practices, and tools. Here, the motivation is not to get attention from those higher up on the chain of command but, rather, to contribute to a conversation that helps the individual as well as the group. In this case, the "knowledge management" is bottom-up, enthusiastic, and voluntary.

A hybrid of top-down and bottom-up is the Center from Army Lessons Learned (CALL) which is using Microsoft SharePoint to catalog insights and ideas from field personnel. However, most people in the field don't have the time to record their ideas. So the Army created a team of 200 analysts to spend time in the field and identify ideas that should be shared in the CALL system.[4]

There are pluses and minuses to both approaches (top-down and bottom-up)—and both will continue to play a part in KM in the future. The important thing in your own company is to ensure that there are platforms and systems that enable and encourage the sharing of knowledge. This knowledge is a rich raw material for performance and innovation. However, it is important to remember that this is raw knowledge. If you think back to the last chapter, you will recall that the lowest value knowledge assets are the recorded knowledge products. Captured knowledge is helpful, but applied knowledge is where the real action occurs.

New Horizons for Process

Most internal processes in today's organizations already have been automated to one degree or another. There are software programs for accounting, enterprise resource management, risk management, human resources management, performance management, and many, many others. That doesn't mean that this automation is complete. Quite to the contrary, companies at every level still have a multitude of opportunities to standardize, automate, and optimize their most internal processes.

And there are also new horizons where automation has only just begun: backward through the supply chain and forward in customer-facing systems. Both of these directions will take companies outside their organizations—in technical terms, outside the firewall that protects internal systems from external threats. The growing importance of relationship capital to the overall success of an organization is driving these moves.

The kinds of reputational disasters that we described above at Nike, Mattel, and Kellogg were ultimately about poor process in these companies and in their suppliers' companies. The suppliers should have had better quality controls and the multinationals should have had better audit and oversight processes to prevent these problems.

Some of the automation of the supply chain will have to come through cooperative industry efforts. The volume of transactions in the global supply chain has grown from $10 billion a day in the 1970s to $10 billion a second today. Right now, each company keeps track of its own information flow. In one of the monthly conference calls that Mary hosts for the Intangible Asset Finance Society, Robert Rittereiser of Zhi Verden described his experiences in the 1970s with the creation of a centralized clearing house on Wall Street when the volume of trades grew too large for the current system to handle. He predicted a similar approach in the future for global trading.[5]

The other horizon for new automation and processes is forward to the end user or customer. Two sources helped us understand this opportunity. The first was *Lean Solutions*, written by James P. Womack and Daniel T. Jones. These leaders in lean thinking cut their teeth in process improvement in a manufacturing setting. But in this book, they turn their sights on the customer experience, providing case studies of what it is like for you to get your car repaired, get a doctor's appointment, and buy electronics, among others. Their point is that most corporate improvement efforts have focused on the corporation and its cost structure. Cost and time in corporate processes have been eliminated by pushing them onto already-overloaded consumers. The new frontier in their view is the customer's experience and their cost (in terms of time, frustration, and dollars) to do business with you.

The second was a presentation given by Irving Wladawsky-Berger at the U.S. National Academies Conference on Intangible Assets in June 2008 (one of the first U.S. conferences on intangibles). Wladawsky-Berger, who works at IBM and MIT, pointed out that so much of the work in information technology done to date was in the back office, where you are dealing with machines and products (tangibles). Future work will be in market-facing solutions where you are dealing with people and services (intangibles)—a much more complex and dynamic task. Solutions here will include decision management, social networking, and collaborative innovation.[6]

BUSINESS RECIPE

We learned about this last category of knowledge assets from our colleagues in Sweden. If you just look at the three traditional categories of knowledge assets—human, relationship, and structural knowledge—you still haven't addressed how this is a business. By adding this fourth category, you will be able to identify the shared knowledge, experience, and vision of the organization as it has been translated into a business model. The next chapter will show you how to do this and Part III, the last part of this book, will show you that business recipe can also serve as a measuring stick for the strength and outlook of the other categories of knowledge raw materials.

Business recipe is basically a combination of your market opportunity and your organization's strategy to take advantage of that opportunity. The viability of your market can be judged by traditional tools already in the hands of most businesspeople to analyze its size, outlook, segmentation, and barriers to entry. The factors driving demand include customer needs and demographics, price, and technological change. Strategy is how you organize yourself to take advantage of the opportunity. As you will see in Part II, the nature of strategy is changing as emergent strategies—innovations—become more and more important.

CONCLUSION

This chapter has helped you break down an amorphous concept, knowledge, into identifiable components of your business: human capital, relationship capital, structural capital, and business recipe. In the next chapter, we'll show you how all of these components fit together and help you build a model of your organization's knowledge factory.

EXERCISE

Where is knowledge distributed in your organization?

- What are the key competencies of your employees?
- What are the key customer, vendor, and partner relationships of your organization?
- What are your key categories of IP: patents, trademarks, writings, formulas, trade secrets?
- What are the key value creation processes through which you create value for your customers and get paid?

You can download a worksheet for this exercise at www.intangiblecapitalbook.com.

Intangible Capital Is the New Factory

Factory
The core of the tangible economy is the factory. Simply put, a factory is a building where production equipment converts raw material into finished goods. Companies make their money by selling these finished goods. The story of the tangible economy is the story of organizing and running these factories.

The modern knowledge business can also be understood as a factory, a place where the knowledge raw materials get put to work. This factory is where you create value for customers and make money. The story of the intangible economy is the story of organizing and running the knowledge factory in combination with physical processes. Thus far, we have shown you that you are already getting paid for what you know. We have helped you identify where that knowledge is hidden in your organization. Now it's time to pull it all together.

The combination of all the intangibles in an organization is intangible capital (IC), sometimes also called intellectual capital. We see IC as a system which is what led us to the creation of the concept of the knowledge factory. By getting you to think of your knowledge assets—your intangible capital—as a factory, we want to get inside your head and change the way you think about your business—hopefully forever. Developing a visual image of your knowledge assets is an important but missing link between the vague understanding most businesspeople already have about the importance of knowledge and their ability to realize the full potential of the knowledge already resident in their organizations.

In this chapter you will learn how to use the inventory of knowledge assets from the previous chapter to create a model of your knowledge factory. We'll explain why this visualization is so important and we'll begin to introduce you to some of the foundational concepts that will influence you as you learn to measure and manage your knowledge intangibles in the rest of the book.

THE PROBLEM

When we were bankers, one of the required parts of our jobs was a "plant tour." Managers would walk a banker (or sometimes a gaggle of us) from the raw materials warehouse along the production lines to the finished goods stocking and shipping departments. Of course, bankers are not manufacturing experts. We couldn't really critique the details of the operation. But we could get a sense of the strengths and weaknesses of the operation from seeing the condition of the facility and the knowledge that the manager demonstrated as he or she walked us from point to point. We also got a sense of the workforce and the level of teamwork. Most of all, however, we got an orientation that we could match to the financials we had sitting back on our desks. The tour made the numbers for inventory and property, plant, and equipment come alive for us.

Today, when we visit a factory, there are many more computers on the floor than there were when we started our careers in the early 1980s. Of course, many companies that we visit today don't even have manufacturing plants—they make their money selling their knowledge directly or through services. No matter what kind of company we visit today, there is always a point in the tour when we walk through a series of offices and the best the manager can do is point out what the people do in one or another group of cubicles. Most of the time, a very big part of the story is out of view, inside the computers on the shop floor or in the sea of cubicles. The computers are the hub, of course, of the knowledge side of the business. And they are (often literally) like a black box. We cannot easily see what is inside them. So our old technique of a plant tour isn't as helpful as it used to be. We still do it because it is a way of engaging management in telling their story, seeing how they interact with their people as they walk around, and getting a sense of how the operations work.

Frankly, the financial statements aren't much help either. As we'll show you in this and coming chapters, the knowledge side of the business is also invisible in the financial statements. This means that it's not just the computers that are "black boxes"; the companies that use them are equally mysterious. Managers and stakeholders can usually describe the essentials of how the company makes money and what some of their key strengths are, but most cannot draw you a model of how they do it.

THE CASE FOR VISUALIZATION

We see this disconnect in a lot of businesses. Just about every manager knows that our economy has shifted. They know that knowledge is an important driver of their company's success. But very few have a vision of how to operationalize this understanding. We believe that visualization is an important first step.

We have struggled with the need for a good visual model of intangible capital over the last decade. Many approaches in use today use diagrams and flow charts to show how all the components of IC work together. But the truth is that there is not one way that knowledge intangibles are put together in a company. In our client work, our writing and speaking, and our continued research, we, too, have been searching for a way to pull it all together, to visualize how knowledge gets put to work. This chapter represents our best thinking thus far. And hopefully, it opens a conversation that we can continue on-line about how to best represent what is going on inside the heads of your people and your partners, inside all those computer systems you own.

Why do we put so much emphasis on a model? Because models, drawings, and graphics are important aids to clear thinking. They are the visual corollary to stories, which are another powerful form of communication. Every businessperson today is so overwhelmed with data and information that they easily lose sight of the big picture. Visuals help them see it.

We actually used guides on visualization and communication in developing this book. Two books influenced us. The first, *Made to Stick* by Dan and Chip Heath, helped us come up with the ideas for the 10 chapters in this book—breaking down the elements of intangible capital into digestible concepts and making the connection between each and its knowledge-era equivalent. The second, *Back of the Napkin* by Dan Romer, helped us think about how to represent the elements of intangible capital in a visual way, a journey that eventually led us to the family room of our house and the tub of Lego blocks belonging to our two sons.

BUILDING A KNOWLEDGE FACTORY

We began using the Legos when we were struggling to come up with a way to model a client's business. We started using the physical bricks. Then Mary discovered that Lego also has a free drawing tool, so now we also create pictures of the models. We start with a knowledge inventory, similar to the one described in Chapter 2. We use a worksheet to assign each of the items on the inventory to one of the four different shapes we have picked to represent the three traditional kinds of intangible capital plus one for products, as seen in Figure 3.1. The only color that has meaning is gold—it is used for any knowledge or product for which a company gets paid. Then we put them all together. There are a couple of ways to approach this:

• Start with competencies. Build the model from there, attaching processes to related competencies then adding relationships.

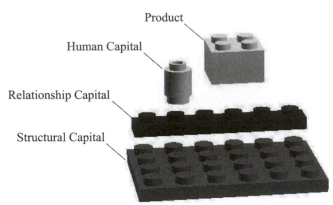

Figure 3.1 Knowledge Factory Parts List.

- Start with your revenue (gold) blocks. Link these with the processes, competencies, and relationships together in a way that illustrates how work gets done.

As we work, we try to link related assets directly together. For example, unionized workers (human capital) should be connected to the union (relationship capital) as well as the processes that they support (structural capital). A product needs to be linked with all the processes that are needed to produce and distribute it. Let us show you what we mean. Below are three examples of models that we have built of three very different businesses.

Google's Search Business

Google's search business is a great example of a knowledge factory. Although it is driven by highly complex math, the business model developed a decade ago is very simple. It all started with the competencies of two computer science graduate students at Stanford, Sergey Brin and Larry Page. The year was 1995. Page was looking for a thesis topic and was intrigued by the emerging "World Wide Web." He saw it as a math problem. Brin got involved and by 1998, they launched Google. Here's the story told through the construction of a model of this knowledge factory, seen in Figure 3.2:

1. It started with the competencies of a couple of students: advanced math and computer science (human capital), applied to the problem of Internet search.
2. The pair built a search engine which is basically a piece of software (structural capital) that determines the value of a Web page by the number and quality of links to the site. The quality of the links is also determined by the number and quality of the links to the referring site. You can see how the solution counts all these links and the fact that this quickly becomes a very complex math problem. The wonderful side benefit to this design was that the more use the Internet got, the more links there were and the "smarter" the program became.

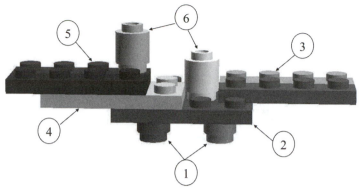

Figure 3.2 Google Knowledge Factory.

3. The quality of the search engine attracted more and more users (relationship capital). However, the users were not paying for the service. So Page and Brin had a wildly successful tool but they didn't have a business.
4. They remedied that through the creation of another piece of software (structural capital) that enabled advertisers to send ads just to people who were searching for their kind of product. This piece of structural capital should be gold because it is how the factory is monetized.
5. Of course, the ad service attracted advertisers (relationship capital) and Google was now a business.
6. Over time, they added competencies and continued to improve the software. But it is essentially this basic business model that has pushed the Google search business over $20 billion by 2008.

A narrated version of the construction of this model, "You Can Grow Like Google," is available on YouTube.[1]

Specialty Construction Contractor

With the Google model, we walked you through the building of the company starting with the competencies of the two founders. We find it easier to model established businesses by following the sequence that you have followed thus far in this book, which is starting with how a company gets paid. The example in Figure 3.3 is one of the largest commercial flooring contractors in the United States. Here's how we modeled their business:

1. We started with the first of the two golden pieces for how they get paid, this one for the flooring products they sell.
2. To be competitive, the company needs to buy its flooring products directly from the mill (relationship capital), so you see that the product is connected to this category of relationship capital.
3. Purchasing needs to be handled with a disciplined process (structural capital) to make sure orders are made in time, that the mill gives them the same pricing that they quoted on the phone, and that the materials are in the warehouse.

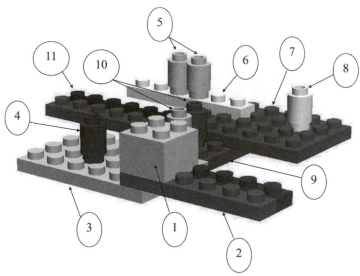

Figure 3.3 Contractor Knowledge Factory.

4. The purchasing should also be handled by staff with the right competencies and experience (human capital).
5. The second golden piece is for the other way the company gets paid, the markup off the cost of its labor (human capital).
6. Because the workers are unionized, their pieces are attached to the union (relationship capital).
7. The workers are managed through a scheduling system (structural capital).
8. Field supervision involves a certain set of competencies and experience (human capital).
9. The installation and purchasing functions are connected by the project management processes (structural capital).
10. These processes are in turn supported by the project management competencies of its salespeople (human capital).
11. It is through the salespeople that the company connects with general contractors and building owners who are the company's customers (relationship capital).

Medical Device Company

The last model is a medical device company that sells a physical product that is supported by a service. The product is used by consumers in their homes. But the company does not have direct contact with the consumers until they call to order the product. Instead the company relies on referral sources. Here's how we built their model as seen in Figure 3.4:

1. The golden pieces are the product and the service (structural capital).

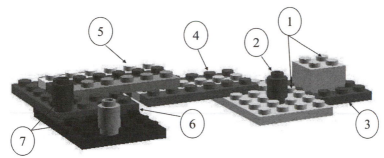

Figure 3.4 Medical Device Knowledge Factory.

2. The service is supported by internal competencies (human capital) related to delivery and set up.
3. The product is supported by the company's in-house manufacturing processes (structural capital). Please note that if the company outsourced its manufacturing, this would have been considered relationship capital.
4. The sales of the product are made to consumers (relationship capital).
5. The consumers learn about the company through referral sources at health care facilities and program partners (relationship capital).
6. The referral sources are reached through sales and marketing processes (structural capital).
7. These processes are supported by sales and marketing competencies (human capital).

The Support Layers
None of these models show the other knowledge assets related to the support services that each of the businesses has such as IT and human resources. Each of these could be modeled as well. One situation where you might want to model support services is when you are doing extensive outsourcing, so that you are clear where the knowledge for that function is coming from. In the next chapter, we'll show you some more advanced ways to model parts of your business using different kinds of network analysis.

BUSINESS PRINCIPLES OF THE KNOWLEDGE FACTORY
Once you begin to understand the power of the combination of your knowledge assets, you are on your way to building a smarter company. Hopefully, the rest of this book will show you how to do this. But before we move forward, we think that it would be helpful to talk about what this model means, what the business implications of a knowledge factory are. Read this section carefully because, in many ways, these principles explain why management of a knowledge factory is different than management of a physical factory. Here are the main points, followed by an explanation of each.

Principles of the Knowledge Factory (KF) are:

1. The KF is greater than the sum of its parts.
2. Ownership of the KF is dispersed.
3. Power in the KF flows down . . . and up.
4. The KF is held together by reputation, not control.
5. The KF runs on information technology.
6. The KF is a business.

The Knowledge Factory Is Greater Than the Sum of Its Parts

When we were bankers, our customers often had to supply appraisals of their equipment. The appraisals always used several value approaches. One was the value "in place," also sometimes called their "highest and best use." Borrowers liked that one because it yielded the highest value. Then there was the forced liquidation value. The liquidation value was always the lowest of all, not just in reflection of the costs of taking it out of the factory. It also reflected the fact that the value of a stand-alone machine is not the same as one that is integrated on an assembly line ready to manufacture products. Borrowers obviously didn't like that one because it reduced the genius of its factory design to a bunch of scrap machines.

The knowledge factory is similar. The best value and utility are created through the combination of knowledge assets. We saw in Chapter 1 that discrete pieces of knowledge are usually not that valuable. So you cannot look at a piece of the knowledge factory in the same way as you would an individual piece of machinery; you really need to look at the whole system.

For example, look at the Google model above. The software algorithms that govern Google's search technology remain in the company when the employees walk out the door at night. But they would lose value and degrade in functionality very quickly if the employees stopped modifying and improving them. And the business side of the equation would come crashing down if the "customers" using the search engine (in quotes because they don't pay for the service) started using a competing engine. It is all a system and it is through the combination that each piece of knowledge gains value.

Ownership of the Knowledge Factory Is Dispersed

Look at each of the pieces of the knowledge factory models above. How many of these pieces are actually owned by the corporations? Not the human capital. Not the relationship capital. Just the structural capital. Even with structural capital, ownership and control can be difficult to track or establish. Only selected pieces of structural capital can be protected as intellectual property. And obtaining that protection, while worth it, is often expensive and labor intensive.

The issue of ownership is one that has caused a lot of people to ignore intangibles as business "assets." If you don't own something, the logic goes, then it's wrong to talk about it as a corporate asset. But if you accept the idea of the knowledge factory, you know that you have no choice but to find ways of measuring and managing your organization as a system of knowledge assets. And the fact remains that you don't own or control many of them. The implications of this fact are examined in the next few points and throughout the rest of this book.

Power in the Knowledge Factory Flows Down . . . and Up

If you don't own or control your productive assets to the same degree as in the past, the power dynamic shifts. This state of affairs is very different from the industrial era when a company owned and controlled most of its productive assets. Wait a minute, you'll tell us, industrial companies didn't own their human capital or relationship capital either, which is absolutely true. But remember that it was the physical assets that were creating most of the value. Ownership and control of the "means of production," the factory itself, was the defining characteristic of the industrial organization.

This meant that an industrial company didn't need its people and relationships in the same way. The nature of mass production made a company less dependent on its workforce. The operating model in the industrial era was dependent on standardization and control. Most jobs in a factory were well-defined. They might have required specific experience but the boss could still tell the subordinate what to do. Workers were told what to do and could usually be replaced. One could make the case that this uneven power dynamic was the reason that unions had to come into being.

There was a similar dynamic with a lot of vendor relationships. Specifications and purchasing decisions emanated from the inside out. Vendors had to meet the expectations set out by their customers. Purchasing departments controlled the relationships.

Will this change completely in the knowledge era? No. But there is a shift that is slowly happening. Organizations need knowledge workers to contribute more than just their time and muscle—they need their attention and their brain power. They rely on employee knowledge to complete daily work and to fuel innovation for the future. This means that corporations are willing to give more power and control to their employees, to give them freedom to get their work done. Most organizations are seeing value in giving more control to their vendors, too, viewing them as experienced outsourcing partners rather than generic suppliers to be pitted against each other for the lowest price.

We're not talking about a utopian view of a "nicer" business world. Just the recognition that if you have a relationship—with an employee, a vendor, a customer, or any kind of stakeholder—and you value their knowledge, then it changes the dynamic. Power is shared more equally in the relationship. And the glue that holds the relationship together changes, too.

The Knowledge Factory Is Held Together by Reputation, Not Control

If you value your stakeholders for their intangible capital, then keeping your knowledge factory together requires more than just a command and control style of management. Your human capital and relationship capital are part of your factory because they want to be. Sure, in the short run, they may stick with you because they don't have any alternative. But they are always free to go. This means that power does not just come from the top, from the "owner" of the factory—but also from the owner of the knowledge and capability. Those who are participating also have a say in how their knowledge is applied.

Of course, if the relationship is based on knowledge you actually don't want to have the participants in your factory just do what you tell them. The viability and value of the system relies on their contribution of knowledge and thinking to build, maintain, and improve the system. You need your human and relationship capital partners to be engaged.

So what keeps your knowledge partners engaged? There are a lot of little reasons, some of which we will discuss in Part II. The best way to sum up the way that you keep everyone engaged is reputation. Your reputation is the reflection of your stakeholders' view of your organization. Different types of stakeholders have different priorities. Ultimately, however, you will have to balance these priorities with your own and come up with a combination that keeps everyone coming back, that keeps them engaged in your organization, and that keeps their Lego pieces connected to yours.

The Knowledge Factory Runs on Information Technology

Something that is often left out of discussions of knowledge assets is information technology (IT). This is a dangerous omission because IT is the reason we are here. It is the advances in information technology that created the knowledge era. IT and IC (intangible capital) are so intimately connected that you have to think of them together. IT fueled the knowledge economy because it made movement, sharing, and storage of knowledge possible. IT also enables the creation and greater standardization of process (the magical form of structural capital). That means that the explosion in the value of knowledge and intangible capital has been facilitated and fueled by IT. And if you want to optimize your intangible capital, you will have to optimize the underlying IT.

In most companies today, IT is handled as a discrete business function. There are a lot of good reasons for this—cost and risk control, efficiencies, and expertise. However, the knowledge of what needs to be automated resides in a different business group. Failure to connect the business needs with the right IT solution is a problem that plagues every business. You will see in the next chapter that the knowledge factory is a series of networks. And networks of people working together are almost always connected to some degree by IT. So the right solution to management of IT has to include greater integration with the operations of the knowledge factory.

The Knowledge Factory Is a Business

There are a lot of people who see a promise in the shift to a knowledge economy of a new, better, and kinder business world. We are actually optimistic about the enormous opportunities out there and the potential for huge changes in our society and in business. A knowledge economy could be a wonderful place where each person is valued for their contribution to a community, where we solve the many challenges facing our nation and the planet.

The end of the industrial era isn't just about manufacturing. Many sectors of our economy are reaching the end of their existing models due to the need for new sources of energy, for lower carbon emissions, for increased environmental sustainability of all kinds. These challenges will force significant changes in the fields of energy, transportation, housing, and food production, to name just a few.

But these changes will not occur because of an abstract belief in the "right" thing for business to do. It will occur because people, businesses, and governments will realize that it is in their own self-interest to make the changes. The wonderful news is that these challenges are coming along at a time when our capability to solve problems through applied knowledge is greater than ever before. Sustainability and profitability will go hand in hand.

If we capture the moment, these challenges—and our collective knowledge—can be turned into economic engines that fuel a century of prosperity. Let the fun begin. Get started in your own organization by learning to visualize, measure, and manage the knowledge you already have. Turn it into greater good and turn it into profits. Don't wait another day.

CONCLUSION

Your intangibles combine as intangible capital in a knowledge factory. A viable factory must include all three traditional categories of intangibles: human, relationship, and structural capital. Creating a model and visualizing this factory can help build a shared understanding in your organization of your value creation process. You will find that you will return to this model as you move through Parts II and III on managing and accounting for the knowledge factory.

EXERCISE

The starting point for creating a model of your knowledge or intangible capital factory is the inventory of knowledge raw materials from the last chapter: competencies, relationships, and structural capital. Now add this question: **How does it all fit together?**

We strongly encourage you to build a physical model, draw a model and/or get a good graphics person to design a picture for you. Work on it as a team. Create a shared visualization of your knowledge factory.

You can download the worksheet to do this at
http://tinyurl.com/youcangrowlikegoogle
or with the book exercises at
www.intangiblecapitalbook.com.

The New Management

Part I of this book was designed to help you see your business as a knowledge factory. This part outlines three critical management concepts that you will need to add to your toolkit to get the best results possible from your knowledge factory: networks, orchestration, and innovation.

The rising importance of knowledge is changing the balance of power in today's organizations. Because they are dependent on the knowledge of their employees and stakeholders, organizations have to learn to find ways to encourage knowledge to flow from the bottom to the top of the organization as well as from the outside in. This dynamic also changes the role of the manager. Leadership is no longer about giving commands (if it ever was). It is now much more a question about facilitating the work of a broad network of employees, partners, and stakeholders. But it is still about getting results.

Part II will help you organize your work as a manager of a knowledge organization. It will answer questions that include:

- How does work get done in the knowledge enterprise?
- What's the role of the manager in this enterprise?
- Why is innovation so important today?
- How can you plan for innovation when you don't know the outcome?

Most of the readers of this book already manage knowledge workers of some kind. But you are probably doing it without a full set of tools and techniques. Part II will arm you with tools that can make your job easier and your results more effective. As with all the chapters in this book, we describe the knowledge-era tools in contrast to their industrial-era counter-parts. Please do not think that we are advocating the replacement of these core concepts, but rather the addition of a knowledge-era equivalent.

The truth is that all managers in the 21st century will live and work in two worlds, the tangible and the intangible. The intangible requires new tools and approaches. But the tangible side of business is not going away. One of the major management challenges of the 21st century will be to find the right balance between the tangible and intangible, the top down and the bottom up, and the inside out and outside in.

|c|h|a|p|t|e|r|4|

Networks Are the New Organization Charts

Organization Chart
In the tangible economy, power and knowledge flowed primarily from the top down. An organization chart was used to explain how resources and authority were distributed. To show who reports to whom. What is the extent of the control of an individual manager? How are resources allocated? Just about every organization had and needed an organization chart.

Our understanding of organizations continues to be influenced by the organization chart (org chart for short). It is a rare company that does not have one. And they are still used as a basic tool to understand the organization and to manage personnel. Every person in every organization needs to "report" to someone to, at a minimum, facilitate communication and personal development. But the org chart is losing its value along with a company's financial statements—neither does a very good job at explaining how value is being created in the knowledge era. The task of putting knowledge to work does not fit inside the neat models that we have used in the past.

In the industrial era, factories were the dominant kind of organization. Although every factory was different, each was basically converting raw material of some kind into a tangible finished product. This linear, physical process could usually be drawn in a standard sequence. And certain roles to organize this process became commonplace and standardized. Most organizations had a specific person in charge of sourcing, production, logistics, and customer service in addition to functional support areas. The way that these roles and organizations were/are communicated was through an org chart.

As you saw in Part I, however, the value creation process is much less standardized today. That means that organizations are harder to draw using the traditional graphs and org charts. Rather than resembling a sequence of tasks, organizations today are a network of connections and combinations of knowledge assets. Although there is still a role for organization charts in management, the network map has become an indispensable tool to explain how things work.

In this chapter you will learn how and why networks came to be so important in our economy and how the technology that supports networks has become a driver of their growth and influence. This relationship between technology and networks begins with the Internet and cascades down through industries and organizations. We'll explain a number of approaches that use network maps to make sense of how value is being created inside and outside the organization. Finally, we will help you understand the implications—and the opportunities—of the networked business.

TWO VIEWS OF THE ORGANIZATION

One image that we have used over and over again in recent years to explain the managerial implications of the knowledge era is depicted in Figure 4.1. This is an abstraction of the organization chart. Like an organization chart, the triangular figure is wider at the bottom where there are more people working in units or on projects. There is a management level that connects the "worker" to the corporate or executive level. As you will see throughout the coming chapters, the shift to the knowledge era is necessitating greater emphasis on the bottom of this triangle.

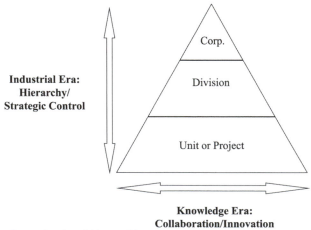

Figure 4.1 Organizational Pyramid.

We use this chart to illustrate the differences between the industrial and the knowledge views of the organization. The vertical axis is the main industrial perspective. It is about hierarchy and strategic control. The horizontal axis is the main knowledge perspective. It is about collaboration and innovation. Every organization today uses both perspectives. We are using these perspectives and labels not to brand differing practices as old-fashioned or cutting-edge. Rather, we have found that these distinctions are necessary to help people understand why and how management practices are changing.

For the purposes of this chapter, it is helpful to think of the organization chart as illustrating the vertical connections between people in your organization. Org charts describe hierarchy. The network, on the other hand, describes the horizontal connections in your organization. This is also the knowledge perspective.

NETWORKS IN THE ORGANIZATION

The concept of networks in the organization is not new. Human beings have always found ways to connect with each other through tribes, associations, work groups and many other types of networks. What is new is the speed and ease with which networks can be formed thanks to information technology (IT). As we have discussed in earlier chapters, it can be hard to separate the history of the technologies that have enabled the growth and capture of knowledge from the knowledge itself. Nowhere is this relationship more clear than with networks. IT helps us create powerful connections between people and organizations. And these connections, these relationships, take on a life of their own.

So we have to understand networks as both a technology and a relationship. Your people are connected more often through IT than they are face-to-face. Even more so with your customers and other external stakeholders, the relationship is conducted via networks. The communication technology may include e-mail, instant messaging, social media, collaborative software platforms, and/or integrated, automated processes. In this world, where knowledge is exchanged and built inside computer systems and networks, it is getting increasingly impossible to separate IT and intangible capital (IC).

Realization of this has been growing. We knew that there had been a sea change when we received a call in 2009 from a reader of Mary's blog, a manager of a Microsoft SharePoint installation asking for help. SharePoint is a platform for knowledge exchange and management. His organization had asked him how he could help them "use IT to optimize our intangible capital." Their words, not ours. In some ways, this is the essence of the opportunity created by networking technologies and the goal of this book.

As we explained in Chapter 2, enormous advances have already occurred in the automation of knowledge work inside organizations. The computers inside the organization have long been connected with each other in electronic networks that help workers share information and collaborate in their work. This is often referred to as networking inside the firewall, the hardware and software systems that protect the network from external intrusions.

Many companies have also extended their networks to close partners. This did—and often still does—require a physical or dedicated connection. Suppliers to Wal-Mart, for example, have been connected into its supply chain systems for close to two decades, a system that moved to Internet delivery in 1992.[1] In fact, although there are still opportunities for automating inside the firewall, much of the innovation in information technology will be in automating backward into the supply chain and forward to provide better service and connection with customers. This will be more feasible due to the Internet.

A HISTORICAL CONTEXT

The ability of people and organizations to connect with each other and to form networks moved into hyperdrive with the rise of the über network of our time, the Internet. Peter Drucker, one of the leading management thinkers of the last 50 years, highlighted the importance of the Internet by putting it into historical context.[2]

He explained that during the first 60 years after the invention of the printing press in 1455, the technology was used to print titles that had been reproduced by hand for centuries, mostly religious tracts and writings from ancient Rome and Greece. The new technology didn't change what was done, just how it was done. Then Luther translated the Bible into German. Machiavelli wrote *The Prince*. All of a sudden, books were available in local languages. They made knowledge accessible to a much greater audience. The secular book (and later secular theater, too) was born and changed society in so many ways, leading to new institutions such as the Jesuits, the first modern navy, and the nation-state.

The industrial revolution followed a similar pattern. For the first 40 or so years after the commercialization of the steam engine, it was used to perform tasks that had been done before by hand: spinning cotton, metalworking, papermaking, and leather tanning, to name a few. The technology provided huge efficiencies and led to incredible growth. But, Drucker asserts, these changes were nothing when compared with the invention of the railroad locomotive. All of a sudden, the technology of the steam engine created a new world. It tied together nations. It facilitated an unprecedented level of commerce. The world grew instantly smaller and more connected. This was the breakthrough that opened the floodgates to a wave of innovations as diverse as telegraphs, photography, vaccinations, and sewers. New institutions arose such as postal services, daily newspapers, and commercial banking.

Drucker made the case that the information revolution is following this historical pattern. The first computers were invented in the middle of the 20th century and caused unprecedented developments. Work and information of all kinds were automated. But it was mainly work that had previously been done by hand such as the creation of documents, financial accounting, and the design of buildings. But the Internet was a revolutionary application of the computer. As with the railroad engine, the Internet made the world smaller. It made connections and communication instant. And it will change our world as dramatically as the printing press and the railroad did in prior eras. The floodgates are open. In the last few years, the Internet has disrupted the very publishing media launched in the 15th century. We have seen the rise of social media that is changing how people communicate on a personal and professional level. This new form of two-way communication is changing how organizations design products, market, sell, and manage their businesses. The innovation has just begun. And the driver is the rise of the networked world.

TODAY'S INTERNET

The Internet is essentially an open network accessible by anyone and everyone. In the space of a few years, it has connected the globe in a way that the railroads and cars and planes invented in the industrial era never could. Today, it is possible to fly anywhere in the world. But it still takes time and money. Moving things is still subject to physical limitations.

But moving information is essentially free for an individual with an Internet connection and still relatively cheap for organizations with larger amounts of data. There are still physical limitations: much of the Internet is still a physical thing—it is made up of millions of computers connected through physical cables to millions of routers. But it is a distributed model that is deliberately flexible.

The Internet was originally designed this way as a protection against attack of U.S. defenses. The idea was that if one section of the Internet were destroyed or disabled, the system could still function. It is the genius of it that despite the influence of corporations, governments, and interest groups of all kinds, the Internet remains essentially an open system. There are obviously exceptions and threats to this but, up to now, the design has kept any one group from controlling the Internet. And it has created a whole new set of opportunities that are still being discovered and invented.

WHAT'S NEXT?

The Internet is one huge network. But it is also the platform on which many smaller networks can be formed. Since we are so close to the dawn of the Internet, we do not yet even understand its full potential, although many new uses are already emerging. A great example of this is the concept of social media. Social media is a new category of communication. It is manifesting itself in many ways: networking sites, sites to share different kinds of content, and sites to co-create content. There are open versions of all these. LinkedIn and Facebook are examples of on-line communities where people create personal networks (for business or personal reasons) to connect, share information, and communicate with their contacts or friends. YouTube is an open site to share video content. Wikipedia is an open site that is creating an encyclopedia of everything. There are millions of blogs on the Internet where people share their thoughts in written, spoken, or video form.

Social media is accelerating the shift from a top-down to a bottom-up model all across society. It was seen in the victory of Barack Obama in 2008 in part on the strength of an Internet-enabled grassroots campaign. It is seen every time a YouTube video creates headaches or opportunities for corporate marketers. Indeed, more and more of these tools are being used by businesses to connect with their own networks and, if you will, strengthen the connection of their knowledge factory. They are already changing how companies communicate with their stakeholders, as you will see in Part III.

The Internet is ultimately about sharing knowledge, making connections, and collaborating to put knowledge to work. This makes it the platform for much of what your organization will do in coming years. But the Internet is the exception to the rule as networks go. Most networks are smaller, with limited size and, usually, a specific purpose. Every organization today is itself a network that is made up of many smaller networks. This means that, without a doubt, you need to understand networks. That is the main goal of this chapter—to help you think of your organization as a network, your people as participants in networks, and your work processes themselves as networks. We'll describe each of these network perspectives in a little more detail.

MAPPING THE ORGANIZATIONAL NETWORK

In Chapter 3, we showed you how to use Legos to model your knowledge factory. This reflects our view of knowledge, or more specifically, intangible capital, as acting like a network. This form of model shows the unique combination that your organization creates by connecting human and relationship capital through structural capital. The models we build focus primarily on the value creation process (how you get paid) but, as we mentioned in Chapter 3, there is also a set of support processes that all companies use. Traditionally, these support processes were built and supplied within the "walls" of the corporation. They would be manifested in internal competencies and structural capital. However, many kinds of support processes are now outsourced. So they would be depicted as a piece of relationship capital.

The model of your knowledge factory is a good place to start in understanding and identifying the networks within your organization. As you saw in the examples in Chapter 3, the knowledge factory includes a series of processes (structural capital) that bridge human and relationship capital. Each one of these processes is essentially its own network. In the medical device company, for example, the sales process (structural capital) involves internal competencies (human capital) as well as referral sources, program partners, and the ultimate customers (three different kinds of relationship capital). The knowledge factory model explains how the structural, human, and relationship capital fit together on a macro level. Just understanding this model is important. It is also helpful in developing different kinds of management information, as we describe Part III.

However, if you want to understand and possibly influence how an individual process works, you will need to do a deeper dive. Here, a graphical approach is also helpful. For this reason, network analysis is becoming more and more popular as a tool to "see" how work is getting done in the organization. We'll show you two approaches to modeling networks to support this kind of thinking.

MAPPING WORK IN A NETWORK

The first approach takes the perspective of the knowledge factory down one more level of detail. Rather than dealing with human capital as competencies (as we have thus far), it looks at the roles people play in your organization. This is the Value Network methodology described by Verna Allee in *The Future of Knowledge.*[3] This approach involves mapping a network where a specific task or process occurs. The nodes in this network are "roles." A role speaks to the specific function that a person is playing. This is not their title on an org chart—it is usually more descriptive—such as advisor, buyer, designer, marketer, mentor, partner, or problem solver. It is common for a person to serve in more than one role.

Once you identify the roles, then all the different "exchanges" between roles are catalogued and mapped. An effort is made to identify both tangible and intangible exchanges. Delivery of a product, document, or money is a tangible exchange. An intangible exchange is something like the sharing of knowledge, an introduction to someone else or personal support. Generally, the tangible exchanges are more formal. The intangible, while less structured, can be critical in creating trust and facilitating better communication in an organization.

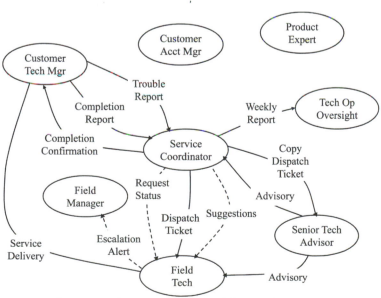

Figure 4.2 Value Network Excerpt. (Adapted from Value Networks LLC.)

An excerpt of a Value Network map is seen in Figure 4.2. This map was developed to improve the process for handling complex technology repairs at a large utility company. The excerpt shows the sequence of activity that takes over once a problem has been reported and documented. Solid arrows show tangible exchanges and dotted line arrows show intangible exchanges. The first step is for the Service Coordinator to send the Field Technician a dispatch ticket (tangible) and suggestions on the potential solution (intangible) based on information the coordinator has obtained from the customer. The Senior Tech Advisor also gets a copy of the dispatch ticket (tangible) and provides an advisory (tangible) to the Field Tech and the Service Coordinator. The Field Tech provides the service (tangible) to the Customer Tech Manager. If all goes well, the Customer Tech Manager and the Service Coordinator exchange completion documentation and the process ends. If not, the Field Tech informs the Field Manager that an escalation may be necessary and a new phase of the process kicks in.

The full version of this map includes upfront agreements as to customer expectations and commitments on service-level agreements. There is also a set of procedures for escalating problems that cannot be resolved through the initial work of the Field Tech. The analysis found a number of places in the process where responsibility shifted from one person to another but the person receiving the handoff wasn't getting full information. Communication flows for these handoffs were improved. The map also graphically showed that initial service-level negotiations were handled without input from the field which often led to agreements that did not work well in reality. Small work groups were able to make dramatic progress in the span of just a few weeks.

The power of this approach is that the map is created by the people who do the work that is being mapped. It helps them think through what actually happens in their everyday work—and how to improve it. Unlike pure process maps, this approach also captures the critical exchanges of information and assistance—the human-centric intangible exchanges that help make the system work. The concept of mapping intangible exchanges helps, we believe, to make sense of the multiplicity of goals and benefits that network participants have in a business setting. It also empowers the people doing the work to improve it themselves. This kind of bottom-up thinking is critical to the optimization of the knowledge enterprise.

We also like the Value Networks LLC organization as a case study for operationalization of knowledge and its 21st-century business model. From its beginnings in the mid-1990s, the methodology has been developed into both an open source and commercial offering. There is also a software package that facilitates the analysis and visualization of the network maps. Rather than trying to keep the methodology as a proprietary offering, the group is maximizing its reach and impact by empowering people on the line inside organizations to model and optimize their own work.

MAPPING PERSONAL NETWORKS

A second way to approach network analysis within the knowledge factory is to zoom down to the level of individual workers. One of the common ways of using this kind of map is to identify and find patterns in the interaction between groups of employees and/or groups of external people. This kind of analysis can be used to identify critical sources of knowledge, the "go-to" people to find information or solve problems. It can also be used to understand the knowledge exchanges that happen—who helps connect people together, who helps solve problems, and who has specialized knowledge.

A simple but very clear example of this kind of analysis was published a number of years ago by some of the leaders in the field of social network analysis in an article entitled, "Knowing What We Know."[4] It described a company that had made significant investment in knowledge management technologies. Within this company, there was a large division whose organization chart is illustrated in Figure 4.3. In the research described, the flow of information within this division was examined. It produced a very different pattern from the org chart. The map of the social network among this group, shown in Figure 4.4, makes it clear that a midlevel manager, Cole, was very important to the flow of information. This represented a risk to the organization. Cole could become overburdened. Further, if he were to leave the organization, there would be a big hole in the communications flows. A key outcome of this analysis was to channel some of the requests that Cole was receiving to other managers. Other findings included the fact that the most senior manager, Jones, was one of the most peripheral people in the network and needed to re-engage with the group. Finally, it was clear that a recent office move by the subgroup at the top had separated them from their peers, a situation remedied through more deliberate communication and instant messaging.

Although very simple, this example illustrates the power of network analysis at the level of individual people in your organization. Much larger analyses are now possible using visualization software. Social network analysis can be done for groups of all sizes and purposes. In the medical device company described above, for example, this approach would mean moving beyond roles and mapping people—each of the 80 or so internal and several hundred external players—as one large network or as a series of geographical networks across the country. Or in a research network, it could mean mapping players in multiple organizations across the globe. The goal of any of these is to identify the quantity of information flows and the role played by individuals in the network.

PUTTING NETWORKS TO USE

In all these discussions on the growth of networks and organizations, it is hard to say which came first—the human or the technological connection. The shift to a knowledge economy has made it more and more attractive to connect and automate using IT and networking technologies. The rise of new forms of networking such as social media is actually fueling the trend. Probably some

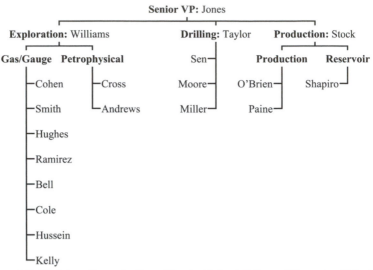

Figure 4.3 Division Organization Chart. (Adapted from "Knowing What We Know: Supporting Knowledge Creation and Sharing in Social Networks," by Rob Cross, Andrew Parker, Laurence Prusak, and Stephen P. Borgatti. *Ageless Learner*, on-line. Retrieved November 13, 2009. http://agelesslearner.com/articles/knowing_crossetal_tc600.html.)

of the most interesting trends are the situations where the concept of networking is changing the whole vision of the business. If you begin to see your organization as a network, then the world literally opens up to you.

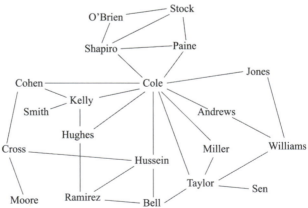

Figure 4.4 Division Social Network. (Adapted from "Knowing What We Know: Supporting Knowledge Creation and Sharing in Social Networks," by Rob Cross, Andrew Parker, Laurence Prusak, and Stephen P. Borgatti. *Ageless Learner*, on-line. Retrieved November 13, 2009. http://agelesslearner.com/articles/knowing_crossetal_tc600.html.)

An example of this is the "two-sided market" network which is used to explain markets where platform providers serve as a connecting node between two kinds of stakeholders. Examples include Microsoft and/or Apple who are intermediaries between consumers and application developers. Another example is Monster and CareerBuilder who serve as a connection between employers and job seekers.[5]

The concept of networked business models has also been applied very effectively in the nonprofit sphere. We became aware of this approach to achieving social goals through a paper by Jane Wei-Skillern and Sonia Marciano. They document how the small, networked organizations can accomplish much more than large nonprofits that do all the work themselves. They contrast two models within the organization Habitat for Humanity. The typical Habitat program in a country builds around 200 houses per year by focusing on fundraising, staffing, and programming. But the program in Egypt takes a different tack. It works through existing community organizations and averages around 1,000 houses per year. This approach puts the mission at the center of operations and is willing to cede some control in the process.[6]

A final example of a networked business model that has been used frequently in recent years is Al Qaeda, which was deliberately designed as a decentralized system of cells linked primarily by ideology. Our friend Ken Jarboe at the Athena Alliance, blogged in 2007 that it was ironic that the U.S. response to this networked business model was to "rearrange the bureaucracy" by creating the large Department of Homeland Security.[7] This can almost be seen as a battle between centralized and decentralized control.

THE QUESTION OF CONTROL

As with so many other aspects of knowledge assets, there are both bottom-up and top-down aspects to networks. There are many who study networks that see them as analogous to self-organizing, living systems that occur in nature. If you believe this, then you believe that organizations can organize themselves. There is a lot of truth to this and it makes sense to dig in, using the approaches we outline above to understand how a network is working organically so that interventions are effective. But it is unrealistic to believe that businesses will become completely self-organizing in our lifetimes, if ever.

On a practical level, organizations often do take a top-down approach and try to influence and improve the performance of their networks—or even to create them. Chris Meyer of Monitor Network explains this view by saying "networks are like computers in that they need applications software or a design of how to use them to be productive, and to do this we begin with the work and not the technology."[8] In other words, networks need a task, a sense of purpose, to be effective. His suggested approach is to first define the work to be done, then identify the talent needed to make it happen, "engineer" the exchanges needed, design the experience, and assemble the technology.[9] In other words, build your networks by thinking about the business purpose first and then the technology and platform.

As we explained in Chapters 2 and 3, the knowledge factory is an updated version of the Value Chain diagram developed by Michael Porter.

When it came time to organize the kind of business depicted in Porter's graphic, the organization chart fit the bill. There was someone in charge of each of the boxes in the value chain. Sometimes there was a manager overseeing several of those managers—a head of manufacturing, or of an individual plant. Many companies also had Chief Operating Officers. At the top was a CEO and/or a President. Power, funding, and communications all flowed from the top to the bottom along the *chain of command*, a term that invokes a military organization but one that is changing as we speak.

Of course, every organization still has an org chart and a chain of command. But neither is as monolithic as it used to be. The work of most organizations today cannot get done if employees are forbidden to reach into another silo or chain of command directly as opposed to the old way of "going through channels" that slowed things down and inhibited communication. As you will see in the next chapter, there is a balance to be struck between the org chart and the network map.

CONCLUSION

In this chapter you began to understand your organization not only from the top down, as illustrated by an org chart, but also from the bottom up, as illustrated by a set of interconnected networks. Chapter 5 goes into greater detail about how to balance these two perspectives and your role as a manager.

EXERCISE

What are the key networks in your organization?
Start with the model of your knowledge factory. Now identify each discrete process and build a separate, detailed map of each of the key processes as a network. Some of the things to think about when you are mapping your business include:

- Who are the players in the network?
- What are their roles?
- What resources do they need?
- What is the nature of the interactions?
- Would the players benefit from training to be more effective in their roles?
- What roles/interactions are missing?
- What resources are missing or would help improve the overall effectiveness of the network?
- What is the role of a manager in this network?

You can download a worksheet for this exercise at
www.intangiblecapitalbook.com.

Orchestration Is the New Command and Control

Command and Control

In the tangible economy, mechanization and mass production drove huge productivity gains as manufactured goods replaced those made by hand. These efficiencies came through strict discipline. Managers could describe to their employees in great detail the smartest way to accomplish their work: "Take Part A, attach these two screws, then join Part A to Part B." Through time and motion studies, the fastest and most efficient way to do things could be identified. To achieve these results, employees had to adhere to strict guidelines. In such an organization, decision making was an activity that resided with management. Like military commanders, the word of managers was the guide for corporate action.

As we saw in the last chapters, your knowledge factory is really a series of networks. These networks include both internal and external players. Knowledge is dispersed throughout the network—it is not concentrated in the managerial class. And the organization needs that knowledge to succeed. This means that a traditional hierarchical approach where knowledge and power flow from the top down will not get you the results you need.

This chapter describes a new approach to management that recognizes the critical differences that have come into the organization as a result of the rise of the knowledge era. It is about managing horizontally across the knowledge base of your business. We define knowledge work and knowledge workers. We borrow the image of the orchestra conductor from Peter Drucker to explain what a manager should and should not try to do to support the growth of his or her organization. And we try to give you some guidelines on what your role should be within your organization's networks.

In many ways, this was the hardest chapter for us to write. There is a lot to understand about the changes in business before you can appreciate all the implications for management. And, in some ways, the answers have yet to emerge. It's funny because a few years back, we wrote a review of Gary Hamel's *The Future of Management* that criticized him for ending his call for management innovation with a statement that essentially said we don't know the answers yet. But when we sat down to write this chapter we almost threw up our hands, too.

Hamel was right. Many answers are yet to come. But we have seen in our practice the value of many of the approaches described in this book. We can tell you for certain that the goal of the corporation and the goal of management will be to put knowledge to work in the most effective way. This chapter examines the implications of that goal on the role of the manager as it continues to shift from that of a commander to that of a conductor.

THE ORCHESTRA CONDUCTOR

Drucker used the metaphor of the orchestra conductor over and over again to describe the challenge of management in the knowledge era. He explained that an orchestra conductor does not know how to play each of the instruments of an orchestra. Yet, the conductor clearly is the leader and manager of the team making up the orchestra. In his or her work, the conductor cannot and should not get too deeply into the technical details of each individual instrument and musician. Rather, the conductor chooses the music, sets the pace, and ensures that all the musicians are playing together. "A great orchestra," he asserted, "is not composed of great instrumentalists but of adequate ones who produce at their peak."[1]

Sound easy? Of course not. But it captures the essence of the challenge of management in the knowledge era. And makes it clear that a new management model is needed because workers underneath a manager have special talents and skills that the manager does not possess. This approach contrasts sharply with the widely understood dynamic in the industrial model. Industrial workers were expected to do as they were told. They were not valued for their knowledge or creativity. Although this is an overly simplistic statement, it is more true than most people would care to admit, even today. Because the majority of organizations are still set up as if they were running factories where workers are interchangeable and dispensable—rather than businesses dependent on knowledge workers to create and preserve competitive advantage.

WHAT IS A KNOWLEDGE WORKER?

The essence of what knowledge workers do can be summed up in two words: they think. Here are a few more: They use their judgment. They apply their experience. They make decisions about what to do and how to do it. They innovate. They contribute their knowledge to the work of the overall organization, just as a musician plays one part of a complex piece of orchestra music.

This is not to say that knowledge work is a free-form exercise. The boundaries of the task are usually pretty clear. Every musician is playing different parts of the same piece of music. In fact, this is why structural capital is so important. If all the routine thinking tasks are automated or standardized in some way, the knowledge worker is freed to apply their time and attention to problems on the margin—challenges that are outside the norm, opportunities to improve existing structural capital, or opportunities to create entirely new forms of structural capital.

Knowledge work is often, through necessity, collaborative. Just as the conductor cannot play all of the instruments in the orchestra, neither can the individual musicians. Many problems need input, thinking, and the experience of other knowledge workers. This happens as a matter of course within established groups. It may be as simple as a meeting or an on-line discussion.

But it may also mean that a team of people may be assembled to address a specific problem. This is often called the *Hollywood Model*. In the early days of Hollywood, film studios contracted workers, including stars, as full-time employees. The studios used these teams to develop film after film. In Hollywood today, the model is completely different. Each film is developed as a project. The producer, cast, and crew come together for just one film.[2] This system is more cost-effective and ensures that the unique challenges of each film are matched to the best available talent.

If it is done right, knowledge work is constantly evolving. If the stage is set properly, knowledge workers will continue to solve new problems on the margin of existing practice and identify new opportunities in related areas. That is the essence of the challenge of innovation and knowledge work: how to maintain, encourage, and embrace this continuing flow of new ideas and improvements.

HOW MANY WORKERS ARE KNOWLEDGE WORKERS?

The American workforce has been evolving slowly over the past century. Over this time, the dominant jobs have shifted from materials extraction and processing to information processing (see Table 5.1).[3]

The trend was constant and consistent over the century for the primary and tertiary sectors. The secondary sector actually peaked at 50 percent in 1960 and then trended back down to end the century where it started.

At first glance, these statistics would seem to imply that knowledge workers make up 58 percent of the total workforce. It is true that workers

Table 5.1 Jobs in the 20th Century

Economic Sector	Sample Occupations	1900	2000
Primary: Material Extraction	Farmers, miners, fishermen	41%	4%
Secondary: Material Processing	Laborers, craftsmen, drivers	38%	38%
Tertiary: Information Processing	Professional, technical, service	21%	58%

Source: The First Measured Century

in the tertiary sector deal primarily with knowledge. But these labels do not capture the breadth of the trend. So please do not look at these statistics, decide that your workers do not fit the definition of knowledge workers, and think that you can stop reading this book. In our experience, it is not that simple. The use of computers in the workplace is turning almost every worker into a knowledge worker. Work of all kinds is becoming more data-driven. And business challenges require more on-the-job thinking and learning.

The classic example of how factory workers can become knowledge workers has for many years been Toyota. Toyota taught the business world many lessons on how to empower workers to adapt the way they work every day. One of our favorite stories was the employees at a Toyota plant who were concerned with the potential for error in an installation process that had 12 possible configurations for sun visors and nine configurations for seat belts. Picking the right parts when it came time to install them was a distraction. So the team went down the street to Wal-Mart and bought plastic totes that could be pre-packed with the right combination of parts. Would you call these workers knowledge workers? We would. Of course, Toyota is also an example of what happens when the empowerment and communication stops before it gets to the top of the company. We'll talk more about that in our final chapter on reputation.

ARE WORKERS A COST OR A RESOURCE IN YOUR ORGANIZATION?

You probably were nodding your head as you read the last section. Yup, these knowledge workers are great. Can't get enough of 'em. But take a minute and think back to the beginning of our "great recession" of 2008 to 2009 or to recessions you have experienced in recent decades. Did your company lay off people? Even if you didn't, there were plenty of others that did. People are one of the major expenses in a business and are often seen as a cost as opposed to a resource.

Why do we make this distinction? Because many, many businesspeople have not yet made the mental shift to understand the increased importance of workers in the knowledge era. They do not see their workers as part of their productive capacity, as an integral part of their knowledge factories. Few manufacturers, for example, would consider shedding equipment in a tangible factory during a recession; the cost would be too great to replace it when the business comes back. For a knowledge-intensive business, it can be just as costly to replace your people. But because your people are not an accounting asset, these costs are not added up in one place to give you a full picture of the cost to fire, hire, and train employees.

We know that sometimes there is no other choice. If the choice is between saving the company (and the jobs of everyone in it) and laying off some of the people, the rational choice is to go ahead with layoffs. And, the truth is that this kind of circumstance can be a wake-up call or an excuse to trim workers who do not contribute as much as they should.

High unemployment was definitely part of the 2009 recession. Although it's too early to have good statistics on this, judging from the number of stories in the press, there was a small change this time around. More and more companies were asking for everyone to sacrifice a little to avoid or minimize layoffs. In fact, many times, the impetus for these voluntary cuts in hours or salary came from the rank and file rather than management. Examples included department heads at Beth Israel Hospital in Boston who led a program to avoid job cuts by soliciting cost-cutting ideas and contributing salary and budget from their own departments.[4] Another example was the London office of KPMG, where workers were offered a four-day work week as a way to stave off layoffs.[5] The trend could have just reflected the severity of the downturn, scaring people more than usual. Or it could reflect a new understanding of the importance of knowledge workers and their contribution to the organization. If so, this would be a very big and positive shift.

OUTSOURCING AND THE NETWORKED BUSINESS
Of course, the lessons of the knowledge factory and the last chapter's discussion of networks means that a lot of the work done *for* organizations is no longer done *inside* the organization by its own employees. Instead, partners with greater expertise or more efficient operations take on an aspect of your organization's work. A big driver of this trend has been the differing costs of labor across the globe. During the past couple of decades, countries like China grew their manufacturing base while information technology jobs went to countries like India. In intangible capital vocabulary, this converted internal human and structural capital into relationship capital.

Outsourcing has actually been around for a long time. In a course we delivered for midlevel information technology managers, we used an article about the outsourcing of information technology (IT) jobs called, "The End of Corporate Computing," by Nicholas Carr. Carr made an analogy between current trends in the IT market and the shift that we described in Chapter 1 when companies started purchasing their power from external suppliers in the early 20th century. One of the drivers of this shift was the efficient allocation of capacity. Carr points out that most corporate data centers use less than half the computing capacity of their computers. It's not just the capacity; it is also about the work to maintain huge numbers of machines. This was an early call for the increased efficiency of what is now called cloud computing—solutions hosted on servers that can be managed more efficiently than can thousands of stand-alone personal computers.[6]

All this is to say that the job of the manager has clearly migrated from being an internally focused role that worked within a strict hierarchy to one that focuses on maximizing the effectiveness of the entire network of an operation. The makeup of your corporate knowledge factory and its many subsidiary networks can and will change over time.

ARE MANAGERS EVEN NECESSARY?

There are those who will tell you that knowledge workers do not actually need managing. This view says that if workers are smart enough to be "knowledge workers," then they are smart enough to organize themselves. This thinking is also consistent with the view of networks as living organisms capable of self-organization.

There are a few interesting examples of a "leaderless" approach to management. One is the Orpheus Chamber Orchestra, which has no conductor and fills all other leadership roles on a rotating basis. Another example was Ternary Software, a small development shop that was run democratically from 2001 to 2006 through consensus (one of the founders has since left the company to productize and evangelize this management approach).

Although far from being a leaderless organization, Cisco is an example of a company that has pushed power and decision making down from the executive suite to a much broader base of managers. Interestingly, this company provides much of the hardware and consulting that is building business networks. There is a view inside Cisco that the company has to learn to use networks and collaborate effectively themselves as role models for their customers. CEO John Chambers explained to *Fast Company*, "In 2001, we were like most high-tech companies. . . . All decisions came to the top 10 people in the company and we drove things back down from there."[7] Today, the company relies on a network of 59 operating committees to make decisions, a system that Chambers says could create 500 potential successors for his role.

There are plenty of skeptics about Cisco's experiment, as evidenced by a wave of discussion in the blogosphere in August 2009 set off by an article on this structure in the *Wall Street Journal* and a follow-up post by Henry Blodget asking, "Has Cisco's John Chambers Lost His Mind?"[8] It is obviously too early to tell how this will turn out for Cisco. We believe that this approach will be like Boeing's experiment with the 787—a learning experience that will leave Cisco way ahead of the curve in building a flexible, innovative organization.

In these examples, management tasks still exist, they are just handled in a different way. In the case of Orpheus, management tasks are handled in rotation. Big picture decisions are made collaboratively. In the Cisco case, they are distributed to standing and ad hoc committees. So the right question isn't really whether you need management but, rather, how management tasks are to be handled. So what are the tasks and roles of a manager?

THE ROLE OF A MANAGER

To define the role of a manager, it is helpful to think back to the triangle graphic from the last chapter. There, we contrasted the vertically oriented organization chart with the horizontally oriented network map. In a simplistic way, you could say that the vertical orientation in that picture illustrated by the org chart also reflects a management approach that emphasizes command and control. In contrast, the horizontal orientation illustrated by the network map requires a new approach and thinking. The task of the manager is to strike the right balance between the vertical and the horizontal.

So what is the right balance? The short answer is that there are certain (vertical) organizational tasks that will continue to be necessary. But they won't be your primary job. To make the most of the knowledge that your company needs to compete and succeed, you need to focus on the horizontal perspective. Organizational knowledge is spread throughout your human, relationship, structural, and business recipe capital. You don't have all the answers to tell all the employees what to do. Yet you are in charge. How you use your role will have a lot to do with how much of that knowledge gets put to good work. You will have to be an orchestra conductor.

When we described this view of management in the knowledge era during a corporate workshop we delivered on *Strategic Thinking*, one IT manager began nodding his head vigorously. He said, "You're right. I have no idea how my people are going to solve a problem. I try to put the problem into context for them, help them shape their thinking, but they figure out the right solution."

This is then the management challenge of the knowledge economy: how to create the conditions and structure that will enable and empower employees to do what needs to be done. In our experience, we have seen that there are at least five key areas where a manager of a knowledge-intensive company can and should play a role:

1. People
2. Resources
3. Learning
4. Standards
5. Context

People

As we have seen, knowledge develops, adapts, and grows through the intervention of people. Hiring, training, retaining, and rewarding people will almost always be coordinated at the managerial level. The two main reasons are confidentiality and efficiency.

Resources

Another key role of a manager is to take charge of getting the resources that people need to do their jobs. This usually includes infrastructure, technology, connectivity, and funding. You could say that the manager's job is to create the foundation of the network in which your workers will collaborate, solve problems, create, and innovate.

Learning

A lot of the learning in knowledge-based organizations occurs at the peer-to-peer level. Managers are not in charge of learning as much as serving as facilitators of it. When the resolution of a problem eludes a group, a manager can convene a conversation and facilitate a process to solve it. There is also a role for managers to advocate for learning to be operationalized where appropriate as structural capital, that is, where shared knowledge is converted into repeatable, reusable forms.

Part of the learning function is providing measurement. The whole last part of this book is dedicated to measurement. Ideally, your people will figure out how to generate information and integrate learning into their everyday work processes. But, when that is not happening or is not yet possible, the manager may be the best person to advocate for and develop this information flow.

Standards

Managers need to support the creation and enforcement of standards. There are some aspects of operations that are not negotiable. Ethics is the first and best example. Others include standards for quality and processes. Standards are about setting boundaries for behavior and work within the organization and its extended networks.

Context

The final role of a manager is to provide context. To help the team understand how their work fits into the work of the organization. To help the rest of the company understand the team. To ensure that the conversation is not just internal but also includes partners and customers.

A manager can help by holding up a mirror and helping articulate the strengths of the team, to provide a story that connects the reality of the team to its goals and serves as a guide to the future. Some people would call this a vision. But, in our experience, vision statements sound hollow and empty whereas shared stories resonate and get repeated. Helping a team create and tell a story over time helps provide context and not only maintain connections within the team but also make the connection with the rest of the company and with external partners.

THEN LET THEM DO THEIR JOBS

We once had a client, the chief operating officer (COO) of a service company, complain that he felt like he was working for his employees rather than the other way around. If you pushed him on this, he would have admitted that that was the way it was supposed to be. His job as manager was to make sure that his employees had everything they needed and then leave them alone to do their jobs. The part that was frustrating him that day was balancing competing resource requests. His role was to indeed balance all these needs and help the team see them in the context of the overall goals. Clearly a conductor's role.

SPECIAL CHALLENGES AT EITHER END OF THE SPECTRUM

Over the years, we have worked in companies of all sizes to help them grow their businesses and adapt to changing global and local markets. So we have to confess that we have had our share of experience with employees within our client companies who do not buy into the vision that we have put forth here about knowledge workers. The greatest skepticism comes at both ends of the employee spectrum—the highest-level and the lowest-level knowledge workers.

Those at the lower end of the scale often hold back. For reasons of age or education, they may not feel confident that their ideas are worth sharing. They have been conditioned by their organization's culture to hold back their ideas and do as they are told. They distrust the idea that they should be agents of change—they see it as a trap that will send a finger pointing their way the first time something goes wrong. And sometimes, their instincts are right. On the other hand, we have also seen the high school dropout working in a warehouse who had several computers at home and knew as much or more about some aspects of the business than anyone else in the company. Brought inside the office, he became a critical part of the success of an implementation and operation of a new system.

Those at the high end of the scale present their own challenges. We have worked with many very smart people and superknowledgeable knowledge workers. Lawyers and those with PhDs are two of the most extreme cases. People in these categories often assume that their smarts extend to anything they do. They can be less open to discussion of new possibilities and change away from how they do things today.

We share these stories to make it clear that we are not wide-eyed optimists about the changing management dynamic within companies. Sure, the change will come faster in technology and service businesses where the workers are by nature more independent and confident. But the opportunity is much broader than this small segment of truly sophisticated knowledge companies. Knowledge will continue to play a bigger and bigger role in every company in the coming years. There will be few corners of the economy where you will be able to escape and rely exclusively on top-down management.

WHO IS IN CHARGE OF THE KNOWLEDGE FACTORY?

We have talked a lot about the knowledge factory and management to this point. But we really haven't addressed the unspoken question. Who should be in charge of the knowledge factory? As you saw in the last chapter, the dynamism of the layers of networks that make up the knowledge factory are leading to changing roles and the emergence of new roles. Should there be a C-level person in charge of intangible capital? If so, what should that person's title be?

Over a decade ago, Leif Edvinsson adopted the title of Director of Intellectual Capital at Skandia, a large financial services firm in Sweden. A few companies have followed suit. But it is probably unrealistic to expect this title to take hold until there is a broader understanding of the term. And, we fear that "intellectual" in the title could inject a concept of elitism that would be counterproductive in many organizations.

Some in the technology world might argue for the Chief Information Officer (CIO) who, in most companies, is in charge of the IT infrastructure. We've already made the case that IT is inextricably intertwined with IC. So dominance of IT is an important part of the job. However, many existing CIOs lack enough business experience to lead process-related improvements (which is a shortcoming that affects the success of many IT projects as well). There is another kind of CIO emerging, this one standing for Chief Innovation Officer. We'll discuss this small group of professionals in the next chapter. Although an argument can be made that an Innovation Officer is the right person for managing the knowledge factory, the chance of that happening anytime soon is unlikely. And emphasizing innovation to the exclusion of execution would not be a good idea.

Our vote is for a revival of the COO title. It is a function that is well understood. A COO is used to integrating process, technology, and human capital. Clearly there are differences between knowledge processes and manufacturing processes, but the similarities are stronger between the historical focus of this role than with any other. Currently, this is a title that is actually in decline in reflection of the decrease in domestic manufacturing.[9] We hope to see this decline reversed and get attention once and for all to the critical operation of the knowledge factory.

The new role for a COO reinforces the idea that the business of business today and in the future is to put knowledge to work. It's not about big ideas. It's about action. About operationalizing knowledge and creating continuing value for your stakeholders. It's a very practical task. Give it a practical title.

CONCLUSION

Management has always been a mixture of art and science. The knowledge era is challenging many traditional approaches to management. This does not mean the end of management but, rather, its evolution. This chapter has hopefully helped you to understand the balance that must be struck in the modern organization between top-down and bottom-up, between inside-out and outside-in. Management today calls for leadership, perhaps what leadership should have always been: service to those being "led." All this provides context for the next chapter where we will describe the fundamental strategic challenge of every company today: innovation.

EXERCISE

How should you be managing your knowledge factory?

- In what ways are you a top-down organization?
- In what ways are you a bottom-up organization?
- Are these two in balance or is change needed?
- How about the balance between inside and outside influences?
- How could you improve your teams' management skills?

You can download a worksheet for this exercise at
www.intangiblecapitalbook.com.

|c|h|a|p|t|e|r|6|

Innovation Is the New Strategy

Strategy
In the tangible economy, strategy and strategic planning typically occur within a defined market space. To form their strategy, senior managers study opportunities in the market and align the company to take advantage of the available opportunities. The path laid out for a company is usually clear and concrete. The strategy says, "We know what we need to do and here's how we will do it." This is often termed deliberate *strategy.*

Innovation has been getting a lot of attention lately. So much has been written about innovation, in fact, that it is beginning to feel like a fad. But we don't see it as a fad. We see innovation as an integral part of the story of management in the knowledge economy. A lot of it has to do with the dynamic that we keep coming back to: the tension between the bottom-up and the top-down. We have made the case in earlier chapters that just about every business today is dependent on knowledge for growth and competitive advantage. And in a knowledge-dependent business, strategy cannot just flow from the top down.

Innovation is the complement, the twin, to the traditional strategy processes that are already in place in most companies. Yet it addresses a very different kind of challenge. We will try to explain how innovation and strategy fit together and all the forces driving attention on innovation. Then we will move to examining the dual role of management in innovation—providing a process and, more importantly, cultivating an ecosystem that supports innovation and continuous improvement. That ecosystem is your intangible capital, your knowledge factory. We will explain the connection between intangible capital and innovation, and how to evaluate the innovative capacity of your knowledge factory.

WHY NOW?

The story of the increased importance of innovation is a continuation of the story about commanders versus conductors described in the last chapter. In fact, a classic image of strategy was the general standing on the top of a hill. He was a seasoned soldier with many years of experience under his belt. He had studied strategy and experienced how it gets played out on the field of battle. In the conduct of a war, the general possessed the most complete information set of anyone. He had information about the immediate challenges at hand as well as the progress in other fields of action. Using the counsel of his officers, he developed a plan of battle. As it got under way, he could see the entire field of battle. He had the best information and the skills to apply it. The creation of strategy in this case is a top-down affair. And the strategy was implemented through command and control.

The military still uses an extraordinary level of planning. The process of planning is a form of training, thinking through possible future scenarios. This thinking helps prepare everyone involved for the contingencies that will face them on the field of battle. But for all the reasons mentioned in the previous chapter, even the military's approach to command and control has evolved. This is because the soldier in the field has better communication equipment than ever before and the types of wars we are fighting are against enemies that are dispersed. It makes sense to find ways to empower soldiers on the ground to improvise within the constraints of the overall mission.

This shift is also happening at big companies with many factories and installations around the world—and for many of the same reasons. Like armies, big companies require coordinated action, uniformity of production, and a common purpose. This kind of overall vision and direction will not disappear in the knowledge era. But it can and must be complemented with management approaches that balance the top-down with the bottom-up. Markets change quickly in today's world. No one has a full set of information so decision making needs to be decentralized.

The need is equally strong in smaller companies, although the task is usually made easier because the scale keeps those at the top closer to those at the bottom than they would be in a larger organization. But old habits die hard and there is often a gulf between bosses and employees who work in the same office, no matter what the size of the organization. Successful innovation requires bridging that gulf. And the need to accomplish this has never been more pressing.

HOW BIG IS THE CHALLENGE . . . AND THE OPPORTUNITY?

In the United States, the election of Barack Obama will be remembered as a watershed moment for many reasons. Not just because of the man himself but also because of the moment in history. The world economy was in crisis, graphically demonstrating the extent of the globalization of markets. The United States was fighting two wars, in Iraq and Afghanistan. At home, the mainstream press, politicians, and voters had all (finally) acknowledged the urgency of climate change. Increases in fuel prices emphasized the lack of progress in U.S. efforts at reducing energy use. The urgency of these problems was amplified by the fact that much of the world's oil supply is in the hands of nondemocratic governments. Health care costs had spiraled to the point that there was perceived to finally be a mandate from the people to fix the system. There continued to be crises that demonstrated the vulnerability of the food supply. Education, one of the basic ways to develop a knowledge-era workforce was underperforming in the United States versus most other developed countries.

Meanwhile, the U.S. economy had relentlessly outsourced much of its manufacturing and even its white collar work. This outsourcing fueled the growth of China and India. The economics of the decisions seemed clear. The intangibles of the decisions were not always understood—the trade-offs made in the area of quality and loss of intangible capital were not always clear to those involved. Sometimes the best solution might have been to not outsource and sometimes the best solution would have been a better understanding of the financial and tangible as well as the nonfinancial and intangible implications of the decision.

The full impact of all this outsourcing was hidden by the false gains of the financial boom in the past 10 years or so. Rising home prices driven by suppressed interest rates helped fuel consumer spending of borrowed money. When it was all over, it was clear that there was no real source of significant job creation left in the United States. In retrospect, it is now understood that the American middle class is no better off today than it was a quarter of a century ago.

There are two ways to look at this trend. On the one hand, you can say the glass is half empty, that the United States has given away so much of its productive capacity that it will never come back, never be able to re-create its economic engine. On the other hand, you can say the glass is half full. This argument would say that the outsourcing trend was a good thing. If you look at it cynically, the United States has already borne the burden of closing down old-style factories and eliminating lower-value work. Given the enormous need and opportunities for innovation, this means that the United States is free to re-invent itself and re-invent our economy using our knowledge.

This is the silver lining to the cloud. This moment of crisis is coming at the same time that the knowledge economy is taking hold. The transition to a knowledge economy began slowly in the 20th century as computers began to automate much of the routine work done inside businesses. It accelerated as the Internet made it possible to connect everyone to everything; to spread basic knowledge as never before; to collaborate on a global scale and put knowledge to work; and to innovate our way out of crises.

Seen in this way, this is also a moment of almost unprecedented opportunity. Each of these significant challenges created risks for the country and the world, none of which could be resolved instantly. But they also created enormous opportunities. The twin challenges of climate change and energy will drive the search for alternative fuels, new forms of transportation, new forms of energy-efficient construction, and retrofitting of existing buildings. Remaking the health care system should reverse the current pattern where the United States has poorer outcomes and higher costs than peer countries. The food system can be reformed away from the industrial model that maximizes cheap calories using methods that create pollution and use fuel and petrochemicals, to one that maximizes nutrition and guarantees more sustainable production methods. Manufacturing can shift to a whole new paradigm where low- or no-waste production and good product design ensure sustainable products along their full life cycles. Educators at all levels can use technology to broaden access at a much lower cost than the current brick-and-mortar model.

On the corporate level, there are still many frontiers for increased efficiency through information technology—using it to build intangible capital, or as our SharePoint manager put it, "IT to optimize IC." Much of the "back office" in companies has already been automated including accounting and payroll. Much of the manufacturing process has been automated. But there is still room for significant improvements and there are the two new frontiers we outlined in Chapter 2: automating customer-facing technologies and reaching back to have better information and quality assurance in the supply chain.

This is just a high-level view of the opportunity that innovation represents to businesses in the United States and all over the world. We'll get off our soapbox now. But we felt compelled to share this perspective to emphasize that innovation is not a fad. It is a historical imperative. And somewhere in here or in some aspect of your own industry, there is an opportunity for your company. So let's talk about how to find those opportunities.

WHAT IS INNOVATION?

Before we go too much farther, it makes sense to define what we mean by innovation. Most people look at innovation as related to invention and/or creation of new products. Others try to draw a fine line between incremental and "true" or "fundamental" innovation. Both of these views are too limited. We believe that innovation is the effect of the organization creating new knowledge and/or new ways of applying its knowledge. It's the experimental, the learning side of business. You want to encourage learning and continuous improvement in all corners of your business.

We like the definition of innovation proposed by Sawhney, Wolcott, and Arroniz, "the creation of substantial new value for customers and the firm by creatively changing one or more dimensions of the business system."[1] The features we like about this are the focus on value, which has room for a variety of benefits ranging from revenue and cost savings to increased customer satisfaction. The definition also has room for both customer and firm value. Customer value drives the revenue line. Innovation does not have to be a new product developed by a research and development group; it can be a new delivery approach or a new service. It can be a new customer or market. Innovation can also be internal in the form of new processes, new efficiencies, or new ways of organizing your knowledge factory.

And this definition sees innovation as a systemic phenomenon. This last one is important. As you will see below, we believe that innovation is inextricably linked with intangible capital. To understand your firm's innovative capacity and processes, you will need to understand its entire knowledge factory. You need all the pieces of the knowledge factory (human, relationship, and structural capital) working in concert.

A good way of understanding how the pieces work together comes from Debra Amidon's Laws of Knowledge Dynamics:[2]

- Knowledge multiplies when shared.
- Innovation and value are created when knowledge moves from its point of origin to the point of need or opportunity.
- Collaboration for mutual leverage leads to optimal utilization of tangible and intangible resources.

The knowledge factory relies on this interactive relationship between knowledge, collaboration, and innovation. What these definitions do not explain is how innovations happen. Do they emerge without intervention or are they created through deliberate effort? Where do they come from? What is the manager's role? To answer these questions, let's start by looking at how innovation fits into your organization and management processes.

INNOVATION AS EMERGENT STRATEGY

One of our favorite writers on strategy is Henry Mintzberg. He is an academic and is co-author of one of the major textbooks on strategy, *The Strategy Process*. But he is also a gadfly with a real sense of humor. In fact, one of his recent books, *Strategy Bites Back*, has a photo of a shark with its mouth open wide, ready to bite any strategist that takes him- or herself too seriously. In a number of his books, Mintzberg uses a graph similar to the one in Figure 6.1.[3] This graph looks like a cop-out when you first see it. It's basically saying that you will have a strategy but things will happen along the way and your intended strategy is not going to be the same as your realized strategy.

It's almost like the bumper sticker that says "sh*t happens." This concept of emergent strategy doesn't fit with the image of an in-control businessperson creating and executing strategy in a scientific, "business-like" manner. But the longer you work in business, the more you (or at least, we) realize the wisdom of this graphic. Of course you adapt and change and learn along the way. That's the way it should be. As we have worked to understand the implications of the knowledge economy, this drawing has taken on a new meaning to us. Emergent strategy is just another way of describing innovation.

Figure 6.1 is a complement to the triangle graphic we introduced in Chapter 4. Deliberate strategy is developed and communicated primarily from the top down in the vertical axis. Emergent strategy is developed along a horizontal axis. It is much more about the bottom-up and the outside-in. As Mintzberg's graphic illustrates, emergent strategies are ideas that bubble up from the bottom of the organization. Here are some examples from the automotive industry. There are the incremental ideas like we described in the Toyota factory that come from people on the line who make small improvements every day. But there is also the re-creation of the car production process being undertaken by the Tata Nano, a $3,000 car that will be shipped as components to road-side dealers who can assemble (and repair) the car. Or the re-creation of the entire business model at Local Motors, another Boston-area start-up. Local Motors is using a Web 2.0 community to design cars suited to different regions of the United States and a "micro-factory" model to manufacture each design in the local market. You could almost say that shifting to community design is a way of institutionalizing emergent strategy. There are also countless companies working on the problems of fuel efficiency and carbon emissions in cars. As mentioned above, there are opportunities for fundamental innovation to re-make a great number of industries such as this one.

To meet these challenges, every company will have to pursue both kinds of strategies. A great example is the recent success of Apple's iPod. This product became a blockbuster and continues to evolve based on both deliberate and emergent strategies. Apple began this product as part of a deliberate "digital hub" strategy that sought to take advantage of the growing market for consumer digital devices. The final product was, however, the

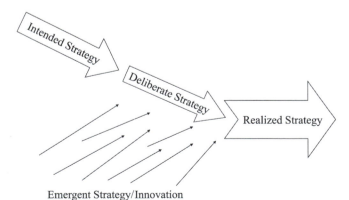

Figure 6.1 Emergent Innovation.

product of an emergent strategy that created a strong innovation ecosystem at Apple that fosters and encourages experimentation. In the case of the iPod, this ecosystem included partners that developed both the hardware and the software. The iPod continued to evolve and the switch to a very deliberate strategy involved getting access to music catalogs, aggressive advertising, and market segmentation. The challenge for Apple and, indeed, all corporate leaders is to manage both of these processes and know when to use each one to greatest effect.

BOTTOM, TOP, INSIDE, AND OUTSIDE

Emergent strategy and innovation are about opening up the flow of information and ideas. The farther we get into the knowledge economy, the more that knowledge gets spread across a company's network, both internally (through human and structural capital) and externally (through relationship capital of all kinds). The fact that much of the important knowledge is spread out in this diverse ecosystem has significant implications on some of the most basic ways that we see an organization. To leverage and build this knowledge, the management structure and approaches need to have room for the flow of information and innovation from the bottom up as well as the top down, from both the inside out and the outside in. Many innovation opportunities are created at the intersection between employee and/or organizational competencies and the needs of the marketplace. Opportunities can often only be detected at the employee or business unit level. Finding and exploiting these opportunities is the challenge of emergent strategies.

The role of a leader is different when trying to cultivate emergent strategies. The outside-in view of competitive strategy is not enough. Leaders also need to take an inside-out view of the corporate resources that create the ecosystem where innovative strategies will emerge and thrive. This innovation ecosystem is a place where smart people share their knowledge and, often in cooperation with customers or partners, create new opportunities for growth. The field of innovation is mainly focused on fomenting these emergent strategies.

THE DUAL CHALLENGES OF INNOVATION MANAGEMENT

A number of years ago, a manager in charge of implementing a balanced scorecard system (more about this approach in Chapter 9) shared his organization's strategy map with us. One of the organization's "learning and growth" goals was "to become a more innovative organization." We asked how he was going to do that. He had no idea.

This was one of the catalysts that got us interested in the field of innovation. We actually did a research project where we interviewed chief innovation officers (CIOs) in American companies. The project, in late 2006, was one of the earliest research projects of this group. We did it because we were curious about the people taking on this task. We were also trying to understand the intersection between innovation and intangible capital.

In the opening paragraph of the white paper we published on the research we said:

> You can almost hear the *Mission: Impossible* theme music thumping in the background. A senior executive steps into view. A voice begins, "Your mission, if you choose to accept it, is to create new sources of long-term growth for our company. We don't know what these opportunities are or how you will find them. You will have limited authority and resources but your mission will involve our entire company. We need you to cultivate innovation to ensure our future success." Such is the mission of the Chief Innovation Officer and, indeed, senior corporate leaders across America. It's not impossible but it's certainly not going to be easy.

In the study, we found that most of the CIOs shared a common set of goals: trying to develop new products or services, better meet customer needs, and cultivate new channels for their business. This told us that most were using a broad definition of innovation. To deliver on these goals, their two main areas of focus were:

1. Strengthening innovation processes
2. Developing research capabilities

This made sense. Process and capabilities are necessary parts of an innovation effort. But when we asked them how it was going, we got another picture. They reported that their greatest challenges were:

- Getting the right people
- Obtaining funding for initiatives
- Making the corporate culture more innovative

These were not process challenges. They went deeper. Right into the heart of the organization's intangible capital. And these problems were not being addressed in the CIOs' approaches to their jobs. This study made it very clear to us there are really two distinct managerial "jobs" in helping your own organization to become more innovative:

1. Creating an innovation process and using it effectively
2. Building your innovation ecosystem

The innovation process ensures that deserving ideas get captured and husbanded from their vague early forms into products or performance that yield concrete results for the organization. Process is the first focus in most innovation efforts. But, as our study showed, even the best process will fail if it is not part of an effective innovation ecosystem.[4]

BASICS OF INNOVATION PROCESS

An innovation process is not necessary for all innovations. Hopefully, many innovations will happen incrementally through continuous learning. But for bigger ideas, you will want to have a process. Just as there are many definitions of innovation, there are also many different views on the best components of an innovation process. They all essentially address the need to capture ideas and track their progress through a succession of steps to develop and test them and guide the worthy ideas to commercialization. But, as with any process, there is lots of room for interpretation and design adjustments based on your organization's needs and experience.

The main components of an innovation process include:

- Idea generation—Stimulating new ideas and getting them into a system where they can be tracked.
- Selection—Having a process to approve the investment of time or money in an idea.
- Development—Having resources or coaching available to those working on a project to help develop and test their concept.
- Commercialization—Ensuring that the organization provides the support for all the elements of a business: marketing, sales, operations, and finance.

As a manager, you want to make sure that your organization has a clear process, that everyone knows about it, and that it gets used regularly. This will not happen without senior support; creating the framework for the conversation is a good role for management to take. But building the process isn't enough. And you cannot order your people to throw out ideas and assume that the process will take care of everything; you have to back it up with the right combination of knowledge resources.

THE INNOVATION ECOSYSTEM: BUILT FROM YOUR INTANGIBLE CAPITAL

Innovation does not happen in a vacuum. It happens inside your existing business. The ideas you develop will arise out of the competencies or experience of your employees and your external network. They will build on your existing strengths to perfect something you already do or to apply your knowledge in a new direction. There will almost always be a connection with your core competencies. There's nothing wrong with that, who better to compete in an arena that needs your organization's skills than you, who already have significant expertise?

As our research with chief innovation officers found, it is not enough to just have an innovation process. The process needs to be supported by an ecosystem that has the right people, knowledge, culture, and external relationships, in other words, the right intangible capital. What are the right components for your innovation ecosystem? Let's look at each component in more detail.

Business Recipe

How you define your business has a lot to do with what kind of innovation happens there. If you have a laser-like focus on a very specific market or product, it is unlikely that an innovation initiative will take root in your organization that moves you to a new market. If you view your business opportunity broadly enough to allow for room to meet untapped needs of your existing customers or move into related markets, there will be room in your business recipe for new markets. Your employees will know that ideas that take you in new directions are welcome. If your focus is on operational excellence, that is probably the kind of innovation that will emerge from your organization.

Think about Wal-Mart. For many years, they had an intense focus on expanding their number of stores and lowering costs. This focus on cost (a deliberate strategy) led the company to become a leader in supply chain management through countless tweaks and improvements (innovations) both inside and outside the company that became institutionalized (emergent strategies). More recently, they have added a set of goals around sustainability, with the aim as stated on the Wal-Mart Web site: "To be supplied 100 percent by renewable energy; to create zero waste; and to sell products that sustain our resources and the environment." Given its size and management history, it is likely that this deliberate strategy will provide the context for countless innovations that will influence and shape the company's strategy into the future.

Human Capital

Want to make sure that you will have an innovative organization? Then make sure that you have the right mix of experience and competencies among your management and employees. Work to keep your staff fresh and stimulated. Provide innovation-related training opportunities, including training in your innovation process. Align employee goals and incentive systems with your innovation goals. Google's success has given them a luxury unseen in almost any other company. Their employees are encouraged, even required, to spend 20 percent of their time on an activity of their own choosing that is at most tangentially related to their "real" job, 10 percent on something completely unrelated, and only 70 percent on their core job. CEO Eric Schmidt has said, "Virtually everything new seems to come from the 20 percent of their time engineers here are expected to spend on side projects. They certainly don't come out of the management team."[5]

Culture plays a part too. As we explained in Chapter 2, there is not necessarily a right or a wrong culture for a company—the important thing is to understand your culture and how to work within it. If you have a culture that is forgiving of mistakes and welcoming of new ideas, you will probably have more success with innovation. If your culture punishes mistakes, a change will have to be made before your people will be willing to stick their necks out with a new idea.

Relationship Capital

More and more innovation is being developed collaboratively with customers and external partners. Who knows better than your customers the unsolved problems they have? If you have a good relationship, working together to create new solutions will only strengthen it. We encourage an exercise we call "Strategic Conversations" with your customers and other stakeholders. This is where you or a third party talk to your stakeholders about how their business is changing, what their biggest worries are, how they see their market evolving. This is not a natural conversation for most companies. Most companies automatically default to talking about current sales or the day-to-day issues of the relationship. This is a time to take a step back and tap into your customers' wisdom. This kind of exercise never fails in identifying a new need or new application of a company's expertise. And the fact that it came directly from a customer gives the idea credibility internally as well as externally with existing and new customers.

Many companies are also opening their thinking even more. This can be as simple as inviting an artist or an expert in a creative field to speak to your people about how they approach the process of creation. This kind of activity can help stimulate new ideas and approaches internally. Some companies are taking the idea of external collaboration to the extreme of posting open problems on the Internet and offering a prize for the best solution. Netflix recently completed a three-year contest where they offered $1 million to a person or team who could improve the accuracy of their film suggestions by at least 10 percent. The company received more than 43,000 entries from over 5,100 teams in over 185 countries. Two teams reported gains over 10 percent and a winner was ultimately announced in September 2009. Immediately after the contest was closed, the company announced a new contest, Netflix Prize 2.

Structural Capital

Hopefully, you are constantly improving your structural capital as a matter of course. These incremental improvements are a form of innovation and can be a significant source of performance gains in most companies. Whether you need to or choose to track this kind of improvement in your innovation system will probably be a matter of scale and/or priorities.

We have already made the case for a separate process to support innovation activities. A related process is a system for knowledge sharing and/or learning. This is the goal of traditional knowledge management systems but it is also the goal of social media projects being implemented internally in many companies. Either way, sharing of knowledge will fuel innovation.

Finally, a system for intellectual property (IP) can be an important adjunct to the innovation process. First, you need to seek protection for the appropriate IP. Then, having received it, you need to monitor conflicts externally to protect your competitive advantage. Periodic review of your portfolio will ensure that IP is being used to its best advantage internally.

Lacking that, it may make sense to create avenues where your organization can leverage IP value through external partners and/or licensees.

CONCLUSION

Innovation is ultimately an exercise in leveraging knowledge. Thus innovation strategy is inextricably linked with intangibles management, with the successful operation of your knowledge factory. All innovation requires a sound ecosystem, which can best be understood as your intangible capital. Large-scale innovation may require an innovation process, a segment of your structural capital that ensures efficient generation, selection, development, and commercialization of new ideas. Successful innovation is the operationalization of all the ideas of this book up to this point: the operation of the knowledge factory networks at all levels and the balance that needs to be struck between managing up and managing down in these networks.

What we haven't talked about in this part is the necessary partner to the work of management: information. Information about the components of the knowledge factory—its operation and performance—is not available in today's management information systems. It needs to be. Part III will describe the components of such a system.

EXERCISE

Is your organization built for innovation?

- Do the components of your knowledge factory support your innovation goals (evaluate each separately):
  - Business recipe
  - Human capital
  - Relationship capital
  - Structural capital
- Are your people empowered to suggest ideas?
- Do you have an innovation process in place that shepherds ideas from generation, selection, development, and commercialization?
- Are you using your external networks in your innovation efforts?
- What needs to be improved in your innovation to be more successful?

You can download a worksheet for this exercise at www.intangiblecapitalbook.com.

part III

The New Accounting

Once you have come to understand your business as a knowledge factory and understand the management implications of this new operating model, you are going to be ready to develop an intangibles information set. Part III will build on the inventory of your knowledge assets that you developed in Part I and will help you create the information set you'll need to implement the management concepts in Part II. The information set you will need is not that different from the set you would use to operate a tangible factory. You just need to learn some new techniques for generating it.

Part III will describe a series of approaches to generate the information that you will need to manage your knowledge factory. It will answer these questions:

- How much did it cost you to build the factory?
- How much does it cost to operate the factory?
- Is it running the way it should?
- What needs to be changed?
- How will you be able to track your progress?
- Why is reputation the new bottom line?

Even though the knowledge factory is intangible, the money that you spend to build and maintain it is very real—so are the results you yield from it. There is no reason that you should not get a good financial and operational understanding of this critical side of your business. Part III will give you a basic toolset to accomplish this using three kinds of data: investment, assessment, and indicators. Together, these three kinds of data are the backbone of a new kind of accounting, one that helps you track the business of yielding financial results from nonfinancial assets. You will use this information internally every day. If you work in a public company or get involved in a merger or acquisition, this information will have a second use. It will be part of the analysis that will be used to generate a financial valuation of your company.

The best way we could see to wrap up this book is to end it with a chapter that explains that judging your success with a financial "bottom line" is no longer enough. The success of your organization will ultimately depend on how you manage the network of your employees, partners, and stakeholders. Earnings will always be important but they only tell what you accomplished in the past. Your reputation is your license to continue to generate earnings in the future. Part III will help you see the path to accomplishing this by applying all the lessons in this book on intangibles management.

chapter 7

Intangible Capital Expenditure Is the New Capital Expenditure

Capital Expenditure

Capital expenditure (capex) is an accounting concept that has ingeniously supported the tangible economy for centuries. It allows a company to apply to its balance sheet the cost of investments in its future productive capability. This is called capitalizing an expense. Then the cost of this investment or capital is depreciated over a period of years. This is an extremely important feature that helps companies avoid having to show decreased earnings in a period where they make large investments. It is through a corporation's capex that the tangible production value of the company (and by extension, its balance sheet) is built and maintained.

U.S. businesses are already investing as much or more on their intangibles as they are on tangible investments in property, plants, and equipment. We know this from macroeconomic data. And we can see the benefit of it in stock and valuation data. But we don't really know on the individual company level because no one counts it. That's right. No one really knows how much is being spent on intangible capital expenditures (i-capex) by American companies to build their knowledge infrastructure.

If you have read this far, you have some appreciation for the importance of intangibles in most businesses today. You have seen the value of creating scalable, automated processes that make your people smarter every day. But, if you go into the office tomorrow and ask your chief financial officer (CFO) how much you spend on intangibles, you will probably get a blank stare. You will hear all kinds of arguments about how you don't own your intangibles, how they don't have a fixed value, and how no one really understands how they work. CFOs will insist that they deal in facts, not suppositions. Hard dollars are the job of the accountants and intangibles are not hard. They're soft. Intangible. "Not my job," they will tell you.

Our goal with this chapter is to help you understand the arguments you will hear from your finance staff and your accountants. Because intangibles *are* hard to see, they *are* hard to count and they *are* hard to value, at least at this point in the development of the knowledge economy. But we have already shown you in Part I how to identify and even inventory your intangibles. So the real question is how to link that inventory with your financial statements.

A large portion of this chapter addresses weaknesses of current practices. Much of today's focus on intangibles addresses the question of the value of intangibles. We think that is a dangerous distraction. Value is not really the job of the average businessperson. Your job is to operate a company profitably. And intangible value is a meaningless metric for that purpose. Focusing on the value of your assets would be like recommending the purchase of a piece of equipment or the construction of a factory because it would have a great liquidation value.

The important question for intangibles is the same as it is for tangible assets: how much will it cost me to build it and operate it? Intangibles investment is actually a piece of valuable hard data that could be available to you and your board and your investors and your bankers right now—but is completely ignored by almost everyone today. We'll explain why, if you are interested. If not, you can skip the first half of this chapter and dig in on how to track your intangible investments.

As you will see, we encourage you to keep track of your investments in intangibles every year. We are not out to change accounting standards; it is too soon to do that. But we are out to help businesspeople everywhere get a little smarter. And the simple act of counting and reporting your intangible investments has the potential, we believe, to be very powerful.

In this chapter, we'll show you what we know about the level of investment already occurring. We will arm you to rebut the value card that many people (in both business and academia) use to justify ignoring the question of cost. We'll show you where to look for investment data in your own company. And we will suggest a path for you to begin to use the data to make better decisions in the future.

WHERE THIS IDEA COMES FROM

A few years ago, a colleague from the Institute of Management Consultants, Michael Egan, approached Mary after she gave a keynote address on intangibles at the Institute's annual conference. Michael's firm built a platform that is used by industry association members to anonymously report benchmarking data. The postings by individual member organizations are reported back to everyone in the system with useful averages so they can see how their organization compares to industry norms. Michael was sure that there would be opportunities for reporting on intangibles.

Our first response was the standard response of everyone in the accounting and the intangible capital communities: you cannot really measure intangibles in dollar terms. But we continued thinking about it until one day the "lightbulb" went on. We remembered a paper we had read from the Melbourne Institute in Australia called "Measuring Intangible Investment," by Beth Webster, Anne Wyatt, and L.C. Hunter.[1] They made a very detailed case for how accountants could keep track of intangible investment in a similar way to the accounting for tangible capital expenditures. We realized that this team had identified the simplest and most concrete metric available for intangibles: the amount of money companies spend every year.

From the moment that lightbulb went on, intangible investment has become something of an obsession for us. Our hope is that this book will provide inspiration to individual companies and then industry groups to create norms for management reporting of intangible investments. We view this as a critical piece of information that could break open the subject of intangibles by giving managers what they crave: hard information about what are considered soft assets—the intangibles that they already know to be the drivers of future success of their businesses. This shouldn't be such a radical concept except that this information is trapped inside of a failing accounting paradigm on which our entire financial system has been built. This paradigm has such a hold on mainstream thinking in business that this chapter will be seen as the most controversial in this book.

THE WAY ACCOUNTING IS SUPPOSED TO WORK

Up until the 1970s, the consumers of financials—managers, analysts, investors, and bankers—had a much easier job. They had three sets of information by which to measure their investments. The first was the balance sheet. In those days, balance sheets included all the important assets of a corporation and looking at the balance sheet gave you a good idea of the corporation's capacity to grow and thrive in the future. The second was the cash flow statement which showed you the investments (capital expenditures) the company was making in its future. This was a critical statement for us when we were bankers because it showed the split between short- and long-term spending and financing. The third was the income statement, which told you how the company was putting its assets to work from year to year. The income statement also includes depreciation and amortization, which expense a share of the cost of capital investments each year over the useful life of the asset.

The rise of the knowledge economy has broken this model. The balance sheet does not include intangibles. Investments in intangibles instead are mixed in with current year operating expenses. And no one knows how much is spent on building intangibles within an organization.

WHY INTANGIBLES AREN'T ON THE BALANCE SHEET

There are actually a lot of good reasons why intangibles are usually not booked on a balance sheet. If you read the first section of this book, a number of these reasons will be familiar.

First, many intangibles (such as employees and relationships) are not owned by the company in the first place. Current accounting standards (for many good reasons) only account for owned assets. A company can only put assets for which it has a clear ownership right on its balance sheet. Most intangibles don't meet that test.

Second, the value of intangibles is closely linked with related assets. You may have heard this one, too. It is hard to separate the human from the relationship from the structural capital. Some people try to make a related argument that a lot of process capital is custom-designed and has little value outside the company. We don't buy that, because accountants would not hesitate to book a piece of custom machinery to a balance sheet.

Third, the dollar value of intangibles can be difficult to identify through a financial transaction. If you have any familiarity with accounting, you know that accounting entries only get made when there is money involved. If a company buys something, the money comes out of a money account and the expense gets booked to an expense or an investment. But a lot of the time, intangibles are created outside the monetary system. An employee learns something and applies it in his or her work. Value is created, but other than the employee's salary, there is no financial transaction.

Of course, there is a powerful exception to this rule. Whenever there is a merger or corporate acquisition these days, the traditional accounting system almost always ends up creating new intangibles on the balance sheet. Here's how it happens. A company pays real money to purchase another company. And, as you will see below, the amount paid in most acquisitions today cannot be applied to hard assets. So the accountants have to create intangibles on the balance sheet, sometimes for assets like brands. But more often than not, the lion's share of the purchase price gets booked to goodwill. Goodwill is essentially a plug number. Everyone dislikes goodwill (except for the selling shareholders) because it is a painful reminder of just how much every business is spending on intangibles and how little any of us understand it.

WHY MOST INTANGIBLE INVESTMENTS ARE EXPENSED

Since intangibles cannot be capitalized to the balance sheet, the only other place for them to be reported is on the income statement. And the truth is that intangible investments don't belong there either. An income statement is supposed to be a report of the operating costs (both fixed and variable) of an organization. Revenue and expenses on the income statement are supposed to be related to current period operations. Money spent to build capacity that is expected to have an effect beyond the current year doesn't belong there. Although intangible investments are generally expected to have a longer-term benefit, they are booked by default on the income statement. Accountants try to take the most "conservative" approach to their decisions and at this point in time, it seems more conservative to avoid capitalizing intangibles.

Of course, this treatment means that income is understated. That's a bad thing for companies looking to attract investors and demonstrate the success of their business. The really interesting thing is that enormous investments have been made in intangibles over the last 30 years despite the lack of favorable accounting treatment. You could say that this treatment allowed companies to have a lower tax bill as the full cost of an investment is expensed the year it is made. But forgoing income just for tax reasons cannot explain what is going on here. There is a lack of understanding and a lack of alternatives available to companies. But the investment has continued. As you will see below, the annual national expenditure on intangibles by corporations was estimated a few years ago to be $1.6 trillion.

WHERE THIS LEAVES US

The balance sheet and cash flow statement should give a reading on the health of the business—its productive and financial capacity. This is a much more forward-looking perspective that gives the reader a sense of a company's ability to move into the future. Today, the failure of accounting to capture spending on intangibles means that the utility of the balance sheet and cash flow statement has decreased dramatically. Without a good balance sheet and cash flow statement, analysts and investors are utterly dependent on the income statement as their major source of "hard" information. Of course, the income statement has the shortest term perspective of any of the three basic financial statements. It focuses exclusively on the results and earnings from the most recent period.

It is popular to blame analysts for having a short-term perspective. We think that the blame lies just as much with the system—the accountants, regulators, and management teams (and the analysts) are all stuck inside a mental model that no longer serves anyone's best interests. And it is ignoring a huge part of the financial story of your business. To a great degree, the rest of the operation is a black box.

YOU ARE ALREADY SPENDING A LOT
OF MONEY ON INTANGIBLES

We can say with great confidence that you are already spending a lot of money on intangibles. How do we know? Academics have been looking at the question for quite awhile. The places they have looked are discussed in the following sections.

Macroeconomic Data

Leonard Nakamura at the Philadelphia Federal Reserve used a number of approaches to arrive at some basic estimates of our national investment in intangibles. He actually made three calculations based on different sets of data to zero in on his estimates: expenditures, labor inputs, and corporate operating margins. The expenditure data focused on three types of investments for which data are available: research and development (R&D), advertising, and software. For labor inputs, he looked at the "proportion of labor income going to workers whose occupations are creative—engineers, scientists, writers, artists, etc." Nakamura then looked at the change in the proportion of cost of goods sold versus operating margins.

He used these three numbers to triangulate an estimate that in the year 2000, investment in intangibles by American corporations was roughly $1 trillion. Assuming a useful life of intangibles of five to six years, he concluded that the equilibrium value of intangibles was roughly $5 trillion to $6 trillion, roughly one-third of the total valuation of U.S. corporations. This is a conservative estimate; Nakamura is quick to point out that there are many kinds of expenditures that were not included in his calculations due to lack of data.[2] Papers by Corrado, Hulten, and Sichel also came up with a $1 trillion number for 1999 which they pointed out was about the same amount as investment in tangible assets.[3] BusinessWeek recently reported on an update of the Corrado study still in process that will show $1.6 trillion in intangible investment in 2007, well in excess of the $1.2 trillion invested in tangibles that year.[4]

The Stock Market

Another kind of data that is commonly used to "quantify" intangibles is the valuation of public companies. The reason is the curious phenomenon that started in the late 1970s when the total stock market valuation of American corporations began to diverge in a big way from their tangible book value. Until the 1970s, these two numbers (total corporate value and tangible book value) tracked each other pretty closely. This was logical because, as we have stated before, that industrial-era business was dependent on what a company owned, which would be capitalized on its balance sheet. As computers and information technology enjoyed greater use, companies were able to create value for their customers that wasn't associated with physical assets. This fact is the whole point of the knowledge factory discussion in Part I of this book.

In recent years, this intangible or off-balance sheet amount (the difference between total corporate value and tangible book value) ranged from roughly half to three-quarters of the total stock market valuation of public companies. That means that up to 75 percent of the value of a company cannot be associated with tangible productive assets. This is a very graphic way of illustrating the extent of the intangibles information gap. However, it can get confusing if you use this gap as a market "valuation" of intangibles. What does it mean when the market goes down—that all the loss in value is attributable to intangibles?

So, comparing net book value of the company on the balance sheet to total corporate value in the stock market does not give you any kind of hard data that you want to hang your hat on. But the fact remains that there is a big amount of corporate value that cannot be linked to underlying tangible assets. Businesspeople for the most part just ignore this gap.

Data from Mergers and Acquisitions

But no one can ignore the gap when there is a merger or an acquisition. This is the moment when traditional accounting and the reality of the knowledge economy come head to head. A good illustration of the extent of this gap was an Ernst & Young survey of 709 transactions in 2007 that showed, on average, only 30 percent of the purchase price could be allocated to tangible assets. Another 23 percent of the price could be allocated to identifiable intangible assets such as brands, customer contracts, and technology. That left a whopping 47 percent in goodwill. Bottom line, this means that 70 percent of the average deal was intangible.[5]

The huge goodwill seen in these mergers is an indicator of the failure of the accounting system to provide helpful information on intangibles. Of course, this information gap exists within both companies that are party to a merger before they even try to combine. Then, when they do combine, the picture becomes even more confused. Given the extent of this information gap, it is not particularly surprising that the average merger fails to deliver the results expected at the closing of the deal. If you cannot even identify what you are buying going into the deal, how can you do a good job managing it after the deal closes?

A MIXTURE OF METRICS

Without trying to confuse you, we want to point out that conversations about measurement end up using a number of different approaches. Some of Nakamura's estimates looked at categories of "spending." But in the case of mergers and acquisitions data, "cost" data for acquired intangibles on the balance sheet (which sounds a lot like spending) is really derived from "valuations" of individual assets (we'll explain this below). Stock market data would be considered "valuation" data because they are extracted from the total corporate value placed on the company by the stock market. You can see that value and cost get mixed together a lot of the time. This leads to much confusion. We'll try to break down the concepts of value and cost in more detail.

VALUATION APPROACHES

Most of the focus to date on intangibles in the business community has been on creating approaches to value the assets. The dominant valuation approach is the discounted cash flow. New approaches to value include fair value, value creation, and stakeholder value. Most of the other traditional methods used for valuation of hard assets, such as comparable sales and replacement cost, are not used for intangibles because of lack of market data; the markets for sales of individual intangibles like patents are still in their infancy.

Discounted Cash Flow

We don't want you to get the impression that intangibles do not get valued in today's business world. They get valued all the time. The technology for valuation is based on creating a set of projections that model the expected future cash flow from the intangible and discounting the cash flow to the present using a calculated discount factor based on the company's risk and capitalization. But this kind of discounted cash flow (DCF) valuation is expensive and impractical to use on an ongoing basis for normal balance sheet reporting. So it is only used in specific transactions such as tax valuations, mergers, or one-off purchases of isolated intellectual property. Furthermore, there would be no point in getting valuations on internal intangibles because they can't be booked to the balance sheet and no one wants to see an entire balance sheet built on management's expectations of asset value.

Because that is essentially what a DCF is, even if it is prepared by a third party. It values the asset on the basis of the expected business model and performance. An appraiser is going to lend a level of discipline to the process but the appraiser is going to essentially use the client's business model as his or her starting point. And the process is very subjective. If you have ever been involved in creating a DCF, you know that there are literally dozens of assumptions that are made that can dramatically affect the final number.

For example, when a company buys another company, they do so expecting the merger to work out well. That means that the DCF is going to reflect management's assumptions about the deal. So that means that the value on their balance sheet is driven by management's expectations for the deal. When the deal doesn't work out, the acquired company's assets on the acquirer's balance sheet will have to be written down.

This situation has made "intangibles" as an asset group very unpopular with analysts and investors, with good reason. A balance sheet built on DCF valuation would not be all that valuable because it is basically a projection of the income statement.

Fair Value

There is a conversation going on in the accounting profession about fair value of assets. The overall trend in accounting is to try to move toward having the balance sheet represent a more current market value rather than historical cost. This is a very powerful argument in the case of easily valued assets where a market or fair value estimate is much more timely and accurate than the book value. This topic was, not surprisingly, discussed at great length in the 2008 to 2009 financial downturn as analysts debated whether and how to require financial institutions to write down their assets.

The discussion of intangibles often gets caught up in the fair value discussion. The logic goes that if you were to put intangibles on the balance sheet, you would want them to be at fair value. Cost, in this view, is old-fashioned and nothing that should be aspired to. The problem is that there is very limited market history for valuation of intangibles. So the balance sheet value would have to be calculated by management based on a discounted cash flow of the known business opportunity for the asset. This would be a management estimate, not a market one.

Value Creation
Some in the field of intangibles, including a number of accounting academics, have insisted that rather than establishing the value of intangibles, the primary focus should be on the role of intangibles in value creation. They have made this argument so effectively that many in the field of accounting refuse to think about other ways of measuring intangibles and the potential for creating new approaches to financial reporting.

We are obviously sympathetic to the goal of understanding value creation—the first two parts of this book are meant to be a contribution to that conversation. But we do not believe that the study of value creation would be damaged by also studying cost data—in fact, we believe that it would enhance the discussion. After all, how can you calculate the return on an investment if you do not first account for the investment?

NEXT GENERATION THINKING ON VALUE
We cannot talk about value without exposing you to the cutting-edge thinking in this area. There is a school of thought that includes a surprising variety of thinkers—from businesspeople to quantitative analysts to philosophers—who say that the industrial conception of value was drawn too tightly. This thinking is best captured by the following excerpt of a blog post by Umair Haque entitled "How to Be a 21st Century Capitalist":

> The value equation of industrial-era capitalism was toxically imbalanced. Why is industrial-era business so destructive—why does it slash and burn rainforests, endanger entire species, vaporize culture and community, marginalize the poor and disadvantaged, and erode our health and vitality? Because none of those have value in an industrial economy: none are capitalized. So the bean counters of the world are free to plunder and ruin them—because, economically, they actually don't exist. Twentieth-century capitalism, in other words, marginally valued pure financial capital too highly, while marginally valuing human, natural, social, and cultural capital at zero—or, at the limit, negatively.[6]

At first blush, this quote sounds pretty radical. But it is actually the thinking that is behind the growing corporate social responsibility movement, which we will discuss in more detail in Chapter 10. This kind of thinking is moving into the mainstream as many in business realize that the huge environmental and societal challenges facing our societies cannot be ignored. As social media and the Internet increase the visibility of almost everything a company does, there will be more and more pressure to consider the greater consequence of a business's actions. Some already realize that these challenges actually represent a set of business opportunities that could fuel a century of economic growth. But the way to realize these opportunities is to stick to the basics of business—and value is not the place to start.

VALUE IS THE WRONG QUESTION

For the purposes of creating an intangibles management discipline in your company, we actually think that value is the wrong question. Value is important if you are considering a merger or acquisition. Fair value is great if (this is still a big if) there are relevant data available. You should be able to understand the state of the art for valuation. We would all like to fast-forward a few decades to have a better understanding of the dynamics of intangible value creation. But, frankly, the only way to begin to learn about the dynamics of value and value creation for intangibles is to start tracking the money spent on intangibles: Learn how long investments continue to yield a return. Get better at tracking return on investments. Learn which investments could qualify for capitalization, such as core business processes. Develop data that will help your management team make better resource allocation decisions and help you communicate more effectively with your external stakeholders. Therefore, we recommend that you give cost and investment a look.

INFORMATION MANAGERS NEED

The authors of the Melbourne Institute paper we mentioned earlier on intangible costs recently completed interviews with 704 senior accountants from large Australian companies. Most of the companies identified intangible value drivers as very important to their company's success. Some of the most important drivers cited included:

Remuneration of skilled workers	72.3%
IT infrastructure	70.6%
Training	69.2%
Brands	56.4%
Customer or member acquisition	54.1%
Executive compensation	54.5%

Yet few of the companies interviewed were actually identifying and tracking their investments in these value drivers. These three academics, Hunter, Webster, and Wyatt, have made a great effort at beginning to show how intangibles investment can and should be tracked. It is our hope that their work will lead to new standards.[7]

But you do not need new standards to do something about this information gap today. What we are talking about is adapting other forms of managerial accounting and management information, the kind of information that gets used every day inside companies to manage operations and monitor performance. The main goal of this chapter is to describe a management report on intangible capital expenditures that will make a huge difference in how your organization looks at its knowledge factory. Such a report is sorely needed because the average company is already spending a lot of money on intangibles—and getting some level of results whether they are measured or not.

WHAT THE RESEARCH SAYS ABOUT THE EFFECT OF INTANGIBLE INVESTMENT

There is actually already a lot of research on the effect of these investments and the distortions that occur because of lack of information. Most of it is from academic research that focuses on the effects of isolated categories of expenses. There are only a few kinds of spending that are studied, mostly R&D and marketing, because these are already broken out on the income statement.

Here's a quick review of the literature. This list distills very detailed, thoughtful academic works to sound bites. We apologize for that but as you will see, these conclusions show a pretty clear pattern. If you want more information, we have provided sources for each. The list is grouped by the three principal lessons learned.[8]

1. The market generally sees the value of intangible expenditures.
   - Capitalized software costs provide better information to investors which is reflected in stock returns and share prices.[9,10]
   - If R&D were capitalized, it would also lead to increased returns and share prices.[11]
   - Customer satisfaction and market values are correlated at the industry level.[12]
2. Sometimes the value does not go to the market.
   - The profitability of insider trades is greater in R&D-intensive firms.[13]
   - The degree to which market values reflect the value of R&D is related to the amount of information analysts receive about the company.[14]
   - Investors in R&D- and advertising-intensive firms can beat the market because the market does not price these firms appropriately.[15]
   - Bid-ask spreads are higher for R&D-intensive firms.[16]
   - Forecasts of future earnings are more accurate if analysts participate in earnings announcement conference calls.[17]
3. Managers make decisions to cut expenditures if it will affect earnings.
   - Managers may cut R&D investment to avoid earnings declines.[18]
   - CFOs will curtail discretionary expenditures such as advertising to avoid missing short-term benchmarks.[19]

Bottom line: spending on intangibles is important to the future of your organization. The market generally understands this but imperfect information leads to imperfect market decisions. This causes what the academics call "suboptimal capital allocation" by the market. Companies do not get a fair shake. Further, company management teams are influenced by the market's view of what's important and they end up repeating these suboptimal decisions internally. What your stakeholders don't know will hurt you.

None of this should come as a surprise to you. You already knew most of this intuitively. But you haven't yet done anything about it. We hope you are reading this book because you sense that you could get better results, get a better valuation, and grow your company faster if you were to get better information on your knowledge factory. If so, please read on.

A NOTE ABOUT GAAP AND IFRS

As you read, we want to make it clear that we are not advocating for any specific changes to the Generally Accepted Accounting Principles (GAAP) that guide the work of accounting professionals and are used for external presentations of corporate financial statements. By the way, the United States is actually expected to shift in the next few years from GAAP to the International Financial Reporting Standards (IFRS). IFRS has not solved the question of intangibles either. In fact, the greater emphasis on fair value in IFRS is creating more of a smoke screen on the intangible cost issue. We'll let others worry about reporting standards when the time comes. But before that happens, there has to be experience on the ground. Our interest is to empower managers to begin tracking intangibles investment internally.

INTANGIBLE CAPITAL EXPENDITURES

So how was that for an introduction? We warned you that we had a lot to say. But we are finally here. Let's talk now about how intangible capital expenditures should be identified and reported. We recommend tracking expenditures that are made with the expectation that the expenditure will generate benefits to the firm for more than one year. This may not be something that your accountants do for intangibles right now but it is a distinction with which they are very familiar. They make this kind of call all the time with tangible investments. An example is deciding between an add-on to a machine (which would be considered a capital expenditure) and a repair (which would be considered an operating cost).

Which expenditures should be tracked? The short answer is: all the investments that you make to build the capacity of your knowledge factory. The following lists the kinds of expenditures that you will want to consider.

Human Capital (HC):
- Talent acquisition expenses
- Training
- Staff development

Structural Capital (SC):
- Process development (internal costs)
- Process development consulting (external costs)

- Software development for internal systems
- Knowledge management systems
- Research and development
- Costs associated with acquisition or documentation of rights such as licenses, brands, copyrights, and patents

Relationship Capital (RC):

- Marketing/brand building
- Customer acquisition
- Product or quality certifications
- Outsourcing partner development

HOW TO USE THIS INFORMATION

When you are starting out, an intangible capital expenditure report will just be a separate report in your accounting system or in a spreadsheet to report to management or your board of directors. Ideally, you should go back a few years so that you start out with a data series that you can use to learn about the patterns of your spending. When you do this, you might want to also gather some demographic data that can be used in calculating ratios. Demographic data that we recommend capturing include:

- Number of employees
- Revenues
- EBITDA (earnings before interest, taxes, depreciation, and amortization)
- Corporate value (for public companies)
- Tangible capital expenditure
- Number of customers
- Number of vendors

The following are some of the kinds of ratios that can be calculated using demographic data.

- **Intangible Intensity:** i-capex /(i-capex+tangible capex)
  This shows the relative importance of intangible versus tangible capital expenditures, which would help your board and investors understand the need for special attention to intangibles.
- **Intangible Capital (IC) Distribution:** HC/i-capex, SC/i-capex, RC/i-capex
  This shows the relative breakdown of the IC investment, which will help you begin to identify the right allocation for investments between the three types of IC.
- **Growth Return:** (i-capex+tangible capex)/revenues
  This shows the relationship between investments and achievement of growth in the company. It could be used to compare expenditures against the first, second, and third years of revenues.
- **Profitability Return:** (i-capex+tangible capex)/profits

This is a complement to the Growth Return shown above and can also be used to compare expenditures against the first, second, and third years of profits in the years following the expenditure.

- Other interesting ratios that may be of help include:
  - **Employee investment:** HC/headcount
  - **Employee effectiveness:** Revenue/headcount
  - **SC investment:** SC/headcount, SC/customer count, SC/vendor count (this would mostly be interesting to compare data year to year)
  - **RC investment:** RC/customer count
  - **Revenues/customer count**

We hope that you can see that intangible capital expenditure data will provide a rich source of information about the value creation process of your knowledge factory and your business overall. The kinds of ratios outlined above look at corporate-wide spending. With increased awareness of the relevant categories of investment, it will also be possible to perform more detailed return calculations on specific investments. Over time, we expect that these data will hold lessons for industries as to expected returns on different levels and kinds of investments.

THE OBVIOUS NEXT STEPS

This kind of analysis has value for individual companies. But we believe that the best and fastest learning will happen when industry or financial groups start gathering data that are comparable among their member companies. We have supported the work of an affiliate company in the IC Rating Community called Innovatika in Warsaw, Poland, that is working with the Warsaw stock exchange to create intangible capital reporting for their listed companies (more on this in Chapter 9).

We also are hoping to create an I-Capex Institute to gather data for industry verticals along the lines described above. This would allow companies to anonymously report their own information and get industry averages with which they could compare their data. This kind of effort would greatly accelerate our collective learning about the norms for spending in different kinds of companies and different industries.

WILL INTANGIBLES EVER GO ON THE BALANCE SHEET?

Collecting data on intangibles investment seems to beg the question of how it will be used. Will intangibles go on the balance sheet? For all the reasons explained earlier in this chapter, intangibles such as human capital and some aspects of relationship capital will never go on the balance sheet as we know it today. But there will be a need for reporting that shows the health of a company's intangible capital. And, as we showed in Part I, an accurate picture has to consider all the components together, including the human and relationship capital.

We believe that someday a greater portion of structural capital will be capitalized. Process, for example, could gain a clearer legal description and, possibly, protection. Think about the package-handling systems at UPS or FedEx. These systems are core assets of these organizations. Although they include hardware, software, networks, processes, and workflow, only a small tangible fraction of the full system is really tracked as an "asset" of the company. The heart of these systems is in the software each company has developed to connect the processes—and how it is integrated into the work of everyone in the delivery chain, starting with the sender and ending with the recipient. The whole process and system is clearly an asset of the company. It only makes sense to develop ways of tracking the accumulated investment and putting it on the balance sheet.

CONCLUSION

There are many ways to calculate intangible value. One of the simplest is to track annual investments in intangibles. This is a great starting point for learning about the actual intangibles practices of companies on the ground. In combination with the data described in the coming chapters, i-capex data will teach us about how much investment is normally needed to create different levels of value and performance in the marketplace.

EXERCISE

What is the level of intangible capital expenditure (i-capex) in your knowledge factory?

- Using the guidelines in this chapter, create a financial report to identify the extent of your annual i-capex. If you can, go back two to three years.
- Create some ratios to understand the different categories of investment in comparison with demographic data such as tangible capex, revenue growth, earnings, and staffing levels.
- Speak with your industry association about creating an anonymous database for benchmarking so that industry patterns of investment can be identified.

You can download a worksheet for this exercise at www.intangiblecapitalbook.com.

Assessment Is the New Balance Sheet

Balance Sheet

The balance sheet is one of the key financial statements produced by every business. It records all the physical assets owned by a company as of a certain date. It also records monetary liabilities and the equity of the corporation. Together, these two sides of a balance sheet served for centuries to demonstrate the health of an organization by reporting the amount of investment the organization makes in its productive capacity as well as the kind and mix of its assets and liabilities.

In the knowledge era, it is more important than ever to ask the questions that have traditionally been answered with the balance sheet: "Does the company have enough of the right kind of assets to cover its obligations?" or "Are the short- and long-term assets and liabilities balanced?" and "Is the organization maintaining its investments?" These are all factors that are critical to the future of today's corporations just as much as it was in the past. But answering these questions will require a different kind of data than just transactional accounting. It will require assessments of the strength, outlook, and risk of critical intangible assets and liabilities. Many of these intangibles cannot be measured monetarily. That's why we think that new kinds of reporting that include cost, assessment, and indicators will eclipse the balance sheet as the primary source of information about the health of an organization.

This chapter advocates broader use of assessment as a source of management information. Assessment currently is used to evaluate employees, specific processes, and external relationships. At a company-wide level, these kinds of assessments provide data that are like random pieces of a puzzle. Each tells a story but may not be sufficient to communicate the full picture. The alternative is to use a single assessment to take a full look at the entire intangibles inventory, the entire knowledge factory. We'll walk you through the nuts and bolts of how to perform an assessment of this kind. We will also share the results of 430 assessments over the past decade performed with the most broadly used commercial assessment tool, the IC Rating. Finally, we suggest a direction for the future of assessments through an open source model.

THE TRADITIONAL BALANCE SHEET

The roots of the balance sheet go back to 15th-century Venice when merchants were building trading businesses that spanned the globe. They developed ways of keeping records for their businesses that were recorded by a monk named Luca Pacioli. His treatises became the foundation of the balance sheet and income statement that are still used today. The model held up remarkably well through many centuries and came into its own as standards for financial statements were codified in the early years of the 20th century. Public reporting of these statements was begun in response to calls for greater transparency following the Great Depression of the 1930s.

When we were bankers, we learned how to use a balance sheet in combination with an income and cash flow statement to understand how a business worked. We learned to trace a company's history. How initial equity was invested to buy land and build a factory. How raw materials were purchased, became part of the work-in-process inventory, converted to finished goods, and sold. We used ratios to evaluate cost of goods sold, accounts payable, and accounts receivable that explained the financial flows of the production process. It was a wonderful, self-contained system backed by standards known to all. We could look at a balance sheet and tell you how much and what kind of debt was appropriate for the company.

But it didn't take long before this began to shift. Although we didn't understand it at the time, that shift coincided with the transition to the knowledge economy that accelerated in the 1980s and took off with the rise of the Internet in the 1990s and beyond. The standards we learned then were already becoming less relevant. Even manufacturing companies began to make investments and show gains related to intangibles. The old formulas didn't work.

Like all segments of our economy, the bankers kept moving forward. They devised new "cash flow" loans that recognized the increased earnings that companies were generating using fewer and fewer hard assets. The income statement became more and more important in that analysis. Helped by the introduction of the spreadsheet, bankers (and their clients) learned to create elaborate models of the future cash flow capacity of a company using the discounted cash flow methodology explained in Chapter 8. This modeling technology helped fuel the rise of the leveraged buyout and the category of investors that later rebranded themselves as "private equity." Built by smart people, these models were and are an effective tool. But they have not replaced the function of a balance sheet: to show the health and the future productive capacity of a company.

You saw in the last chapter the dilemmas associated with fitting intangible assets into the accounting models that construct a balance sheet and why the ownership issue will keep all but the structural capital off the financial balance sheet. Nevertheless, your company is investing in intangibles and it is just plain bad management to not try to keep track and measure the benefit of that investment. If you are an investor, a banker, a director, or a manager, you are not doing your job if you fail to look at the full balance sheet of an organization.

WHY THE OLD MODEL WON'T WORK IN THE FUTURE

The challenge, of course, is how to accomplish this. As we explained in the last chapter, we believe that keeping track of your investments in intangibles is an important first step in developing a better understanding of your knowledge resources. As corporations adopt this approach, we will all gain collective knowledge of how to evaluate those investments using financial metrics. But it is hard to imagine a time when financial metrics will be adequate on their own to measure the health and performance of intangibles. There are several reasons for this.

The first is the infinite value of knowledge. As we explained in Chapter 1, selling or giving away knowledge does not decrease your "inventory" of knowledge as it does with a physical product. If you have 100 shirts in stock and make 100 sales, you have depleted your supply of shirts. If you sell a piece of software via a download, you do not have less software than before. In fact, the value of your software is going to increase because you will probably benefit from the lessons learned from the experiences of your new users. The value of this software will continue to increase as long as the users are getting benefit from it and it remains attractive relative to other solutions to the customer's problem. Your management information set should be able to tell you the potential of your knowledge.

The second is leverage. We have also shown that many kinds of knowledge are free or priced like commodities. Even patents (the most tangible of the intangibles) can have limited value when considered as stand-alone assets. The most valuable knowledge is that which is combined with technology and a sustaining ecosystem of knowledge assets—a knowledge factory. Leverage is created when knowledge assets are combined and become scalable and capable of creating significant growth with low incremental costs. Your management information set should help you understand these interrelationships.

The third is consensus. In Chapter 7 we quoted Umair Haque's new definition of capitalism. In that post he also says, "Capital is consensus: Here's a secret: capital isn't just whatever bean counters and boardrooms decide it is. It's what we—collectively, as global citizens—decide has value, because it impacts our productivity, well-being, and quality of life."[1] The rules of behavior are changing for corporations. It is not enough to produce financial profits. The value of your organization is created by the consensus of your stakeholders. Your stakeholders will also look at your record as a steward of the environment and of your communities. The transparency of the Internet will only continue these trends. Your management information should help you understand the viewpoint of your stakeholders.

The fourth is capacity. There are no gauges on the sides of your employees' heads or your customers' facilities. Your structural capital does not come with the warning that it will self-destruct after 1,000 uses. Most structural capital has a theoretically infinite life. The potential for continued productivity of these assets is a more complex question because the useful life of structural capital is dependent on the market need, not the solution itself. Your management information set should help you understand the productivity, relevance, and outlook of the demand for your knowledge assets.

The bottom line is that financial measurement of intangibles is difficult. This is unpopular news for businesspeople, especially in the United States, who have been raised on the "mother's milk" of hard data. Many use this as an excuse to ignore nonfinancial knowledge assets. But ignoring intangibles is like finding oil bubbling up from the ground and walking away because there's no immediate way of knowing the size of the oil deposit below your feet. We have no choice. It's something we have to do.

CHIEF EXECUTIVE OFFICERS SURVEY

Most managers already know this. Every year, Pricewaterhousecoopers (PwC) surveys chief executive officers (CEOs) around the world. Their 2009 survey asked CEOs about different types of intangibles information. The first question asked how important each type of information was to the CEO's ability to "make decisions about the long-term success and durability of your business." The second asked about the adequacy of the information the CEO currently receives.[2] The findings showed that this information was important to CEOs but there were wide gaps (ranging from 55 to 74 percent) between the importance and the availability of information types including:

- Information about customers' and clients' preferences and needs
- Information about the risks to which the business is exposed
- Benchmarking information on the performance of industry peers
- Information about brand and reputation
- Information about employees' views and needs
- Financial forecasts and projections
- Information about the effectiveness of research and development (R&D) processes
- Information about the supply chain

This kind of question is not as easily answered through financial figures and numerical indicators as it is with the tangible side of business. Yet we all know this information is important. The real question is how to bridge these serious information gaps.

THE NEW MODEL

We have already shown you some simple but powerful ways of generating concrete information about your intangibles. The first is generating an inventory of key knowledge assets. The second is building a graphic or model that serves as a shared visualization of how your company combines and monetizes those assets in your knowledge factory. And the third is to start tracking your annual intangible capital expenditure (i-capex).

But is it enough to just know how much money has been spent? Isn't it also important to know whether your investment is working as well as you expected? Is it ready to handle your future challenges? Is your knowledge factory working up to its capacity? How do you know if your knowledge factory is functioning the way it should? Are these not the important questions that need to be answered in your business?

If we had to bet, we would say that most of the time, you and your team answer these questions based on your intuition and experience. You live with your factory every day. You know how things are going, where you need to improve things. You are not alone. That is the standard way of managing intangibles today. In fact, we have a theory that the rising importance of intangibles has led to the increased value placed on leadership today. Maybe even the inflated salaries of CEOs in the United States. If none of a company's stakeholders can see or understand the workings of its knowledge factory, the management team becomes a kind of priest caste in control of the hidden power of its knowledge intangibles.

That gig is up. It is not that the need for leaders will go away with the knowledge era, just that they will change and actually, we think, be forced through greater transparency to truly be leaders rather than gatekeepers to corporate knowledge. So what will they be required to explain? The question that a balance sheet answered in the past: What is your organization's productive capacity? This is the question that every management team should be prepared to answer. In fact, we will take it further, you shouldn't just be able to answer it, you should be able to back up your ideas by providing systematic data and analysis.

Why You Need an Intangibles Assessment

1. Because intangibles are complex
2. Because you shouldn't rely just on the collective gut feel of your management team
3. Because intangibles information should be the foundation of your strategic and tactical planning
4. Because you need a baseline to create meaningful performance measurement targets
5. Because you may be missing something important

INTANGIBLES ASSESSMENT

What we are really talking about is developing a process to assess your intangibles. Assessment is a word that you are probably used to hearing in relationship with tools in the human resources area. Myers-Briggs and DiSC are two well-known tools that are used to assess the personality of people. Most people in business today can tell you the letters of their own Myers-Briggs type. Another kind of assessment, 360-degree reviews, are used to get feedback on a manager from all sides, that is, those who work at a more senior level, as peers, or as subordinates. Over time, many of these tools have been refined and evaluated for statistical significance. The idea is to use a series of questions that indicate what's going on inside a person's head, how they work and interact with others. Because the output is delivered in the same way for each assessment, they become comparable across individuals and/or teams. The knowledge gained through an assessment like this helps create a starting point for change and improvement.

An assessment of your knowledge factory is more complex than the analysis of a single person but many of the same principles apply. IC assessments generally use a consistent methodology for data gathering and reporting. The focus is what's going on inside the "black box" of your knowledge factory, which can be as inscrutable and mysterious as what goes on inside a person's head.

THE STATE OF THE ART

To date, there is no dominant model for IC assessment. In Europe and Asia, a number of tools have been created by governments as part of competitive initiatives to help train managers in small- and medium-sized enterprises (SMEs) so that they can leverage their knowledge capital. These are all quite extensive and each appears to be re-inventing the same wheel in a sort of knowledge arms race (the United States, for now, is notably absent in this arms race).[3]

We actually got interested in this field quite a few years ago through our use of IC Rating, the most successful commercial assessment in the market. This tool owned by Actcell, Inc. has been administered by consulting firms worldwide over the course of the last 10 years. The biggest advantage of this tool is that there are now 430 prior ratings in the database that can provide a comparison for new ratings.

ABCs OF ASSESSMENT

So if you want to create your own assessment, what are your choices? The main parameters are laid out below. If it is your first time, you can keep the process simple or you can jump in with both feet and create a more robust process that will be repeatable across your business units and/or across time. But do not try to take on too much at first. Here are some things to consider:

Scope

In theory, you could examine just one aspect of intangible capital, such as human, relationship, or structural capital. In truth, many organizations already have scattered assessments of individual pieces of the overall IC pie. The truth is that you evaluate, measure, and assess intangibles all the time. Take your employees for example. You set goals for them and assess their performance. Or consider your customer relationships. Many companies have rankings or ratings of customers according to how well they fit your target profiles or how much potential you see in the relationship. Processes get assessed and audited, too.

If you have read this book this far, it won't surprise you to know that in addition to looking at all the pieces individually we also advocate looking at all the pieces in the context of how they fit together to create your knowledge factory. It makes sense to periodically do an assessment of your entire organization. The one distinction that can be made is to look at the value creation system versus the support functions in the organization. If you have done the exercises in the previous chapters, you already have an inventory of your critical value creation assets. Pull out these inventories of competencies, processes, intellectual property, relationships, and brands. Make sure you have all your critical assets listed. At first, you can limit yourselves to just value creation assets although, ultimately, you will want to expand your review to evaluate support services, too.

Rating System

An assessment involves interviews or surveys of stakeholders. Interviews produce more information because the interviewer can ask follow-up questions. This can be extremely valuable for turning the data into actionable goals. But interviews are obviously much more time-consuming and expensive. Surveys can be a good substitute if they are designed well. In either case, the questions used for the assessment use a rating scale. We usually ask questions using a Likert scale such as, "on a scale from 1 to 10, how would you rate this asset. . . ." But you can use a scale that seems most comfortable for the stakeholders involved. Letter grades (A, B, C, etc.), for example, are easy for people to envision but letters have to be converted to numbers if you want to compare averages or do any other calculations. The output of IC Rating, for example, uses a letter system similar to bond ratings (AAA to D).

Standard of Measurement

As we said above, you already have a number of kinds of assessments within your organization. In theory, you could assemble all the different kinds of evaluations you have in one place but it would be something like trying to fit different pieces of different puzzles together. A cohesive picture might not emerge. Instead, what we advise is to do a comprehensive assessment of all of your knowledge assets at the same time, using the same measuring stick—your business recipe.

You may recall that business recipe was the fourth category of knowledge assets that was introduced in Chapter 2. Business recipe is your business opportunity and the strategy you use to exploit it. It basically explains how everything fits together and how it is supposed to work. If you have drawn or built a model of your knowledge factory, you probably have a good understanding of your business recipe. Why does this work as a measuring stick? Because the business recipe is the reason you have built your knowledge factory and your business. It will tell you very quickly if you have what it takes to deliver on your business recipe.

There are two ways to ask questions in relationship to a business recipe. The first is to tie it directly to the company and its strategy. For example, if a CEO tells you that his or her organization has the best people in the market, you would be hard-pressed to agree or disagree. It would be too subjective. But if that same CEO were to tell you that the company needed five core competencies to deliver on its business recipe, then it would suddenly become a lot easier to evaluate. You just have to ask about the adequacy of each competency.

To use it as a standard of measurement, the interview needs to start with a statement of the organization's business recipe. Then, questions can be asked using it for context. Sample questions would include:

- How would you rate the degree to which the functioning of its processes (or a specific process) helps the company deliver on its business recipe?
- How would you rate the functioning of the relationships (or a specific relationship) key to its business recipe?
- How would you rate the employees' competencies (or a specific competency) that are key to delivering on its business recipe?

These kinds of questions use the business recipe as a measuring stick. It is a great way to take an abstract concept, "Do they have good people?" and convert it into a specific, valuable assessment.

A second, simpler measuring stick derived from the business recipe is the company's industry or peers. In this case, rather than asking whether the assets are adequate to support the company's strategy, you can ask how the performance and/or level of a specific intangible compare to that seen in the industry. Here the score would range from worst to below average, average, above average, and best.

Three Perspectives

The questions above focus on the current performance of the intangibles. This is a good place to start. It is basically the perspective of a financial balance sheet—determining the condition of the company as of a certain date. And it will provide you with good strong data about the current status of intangibles. However, there is real value in a couple of other perspectives. In the IC Rating system, we use two additional kinds of questions, one that addresses the organization's readiness for the future and another that addresses risks. Each of these rounds out the picture of the current adequacy of intangibles.

It is hard to ask stakeholders to predict the future. For this reason, we use questions that target the organization's efforts to "renew and develop" specific intangibles. This creates more specific feedback, especially in personal interviews. Here is a future-oriented version of the questions seen above:

- How would you rate the organization's efforts to renew and develop the processes (or a specific process) key to its business recipe?
- How would you rate the organization's efforts to renew and develop the relationships (or a specific relationship) key to its business recipe?
- How would you rate the organization's efforts to renew and develop employee competencies (or a specific competency) key to its business recipe?

The final key perspective for the knowledge-era balance sheet is risk. If the components of intangible capital are considered as assets, then risk is the way to describe the corresponding liabilities. Weak assets or unresolved challenges can also be viewed as risk. In an assessment of intangible capital, questions about risk are usually pretty specific. Examples of these include:

- Assess how vulnerable the company is to individual customer defections.
- Assess the probability that key employees leave the company within a year.
- Assess the company's system or process for quality appraisal according to how well it works.

Risk management is often a separate function within an organization. However, like most corporate functions, it is more accustomed to working with tangibles than with intangibles. There is real potential for making a link between intangibles and risk management in areas such as process design and compliance as well as human capital management.

We saw the value of using the three perspectives—current, future, and risk—in a rating we did of an organization several years ago. This organization was trying to adapt its strategy to changes in its market. When we tallied up the results of all the interviews, the ratings for the employees' current competencies were the highest of all the components of its intangible capital. But when questions were asked about the renewal and development of those same competencies, the score was the lowest of all the intangible capital components. There were also risks highlighted in the same vein. The finding was that while the organization had great people who were well-suited to their current business recipe, they were not at all prepared for the change that the organization felt was inevitable. This was a very powerful finding. If we hadn't asked the question from the different perspectives, we would have had a very skewed view of the strength of the intangible capital.

Who Should Assess?

If you are the leader of a business or a team, you may want to start off with a self-assessment where you rate your knowledge assets based on your understanding of your business. This alone can be a powerful process for you. But, as with most data-gathering exercises, there would be greater value in consulting others. The next step, therefore, would be to do a self-assessment as a team. The gold standard is to incorporate stakeholders of all kinds in the process. In our work, we prefer to use even more external than internal stakeholders and to get a variety of perspectives: managers, employees, industry experts, customers, partners, and suppliers.

You may want to engage a third party to perform the interviews for you. This can help you avoid the bias of internal interviewers who may think they know the answer to a question or whose understanding of an answer is colored by their personal opinions. Actually, the starting point of almost any management consulting exercise is a diagnostic or assessment of the company. Depending on the purpose of the engagement and the experience of the consultant, this may or may not cover all the areas of knowledge assets. But, frankly, the knowledge intangibles are a frequent focus of diagnostics in one form or another. This is because every company has significant information gaps which they do not know how to fill.

Hiring a large consulting firm to dig around and figure out what's happening on an ad hoc basis is a common practice. Although more widespread assessment will not eliminate the need for management consultants, it would probably mean fewer situations where a diagnostic or a custom assessment needs to be developed. That means that more resources can be applied to actually using the knowledge gained to effect change in the organization.

This is a way that corporate assessments could become a "disruptive innovation"[4] in the management consulting market. A good standardized assessment can often identify the same set of issues as a full-scale custom project. There are several reasons for this. First, an assessment can be viewed as a piece of structural capital, where the accumulated knowledge is built into the tool. It makes everyone who uses it as smart as the smartest person who designed it. The consulting team does not have to re-invent the wheel every time. Second, assessments that rely on stakeholders with deep knowledge of the company have a leg up on situations where consultants have to get up to speed to make their own evaluation. Third, the use of external stakeholders brings an outside perspective which is one of the value propositions of consultants ("we can help you apply best practices from other companies and industries . . .").

Actually, the ultimate disruption would be an evolution of assessments to the point where stakeholders can collaboratively evaluate the strength of the company. At this point, there is no precedent for a social media solution that digs this deeply into a company's operations. But it is possible from a technological point of view and could certainly be managed in or out of the public eye. This kind of social media solution may be the fulfillment of Umair Haque's statement that "capital is consensus."

HOW TO USE ASSESSMENT DATA

So once you have completed an assessment of your intangible capital, your knowledge factory, what should you do next? The immediate answer is that you should use it the way that you use other performance data. It should inform your strategy process. Strengths and weaknesses, knowledge assets, and risks should be addressed. Strengths and assets drive performance and are also the best place to look for future innovations. Weaknesses and risks need to be addressed or mitigated. The information should also provide a baseline for your performance measurement system; the next chapter deals with this kind of system in greater detail. Another use of this information is to explain your business to your stakeholders. Over time, there have been a few companies that have actually published assessments of one kind or another. Corporate reporting is a very important topic that is also included in the final chapter.

THE IC RATING EXPERIENCE

The IC Rating Community provides one of the few available global snapshots of the state of the art in intangibles management. Over the past 10 years, this community of consulting firms has performed over 430 ratings of intangible capital assets and management. The rated organizations are concentrated in Europe, Japan, and to a lesser extent, India, Australia, and the Americas. As one might imagine, the rated organizations have been concentrated in services and intangibles-intensive industries such as distribution and telecom. Nevertheless, there have also been many ratings performed in tangibles-intensive industries such as manufacturing, food, and infrastructure. Examples of these companies include Hitachi, Nissan, Tata Group, Goodyear, Ericsson, TeliaSonera, SEB, and Nordea, to name a few.

Overall Results

In collaboration with our partners in the IC Rating network, we recently completed two studies of IC Rating. The first study looked at the full database of 430 ratings that was published in Issue 35 of *IAM Magazine*.[5] We were surprised to see a clear pattern in the overall results. As you can see in Table 8.1, the ranking of the strength of IC management components from highest to lowest falls neatly into order by IC category; human capital is the strongest, followed by relationship capital, business recipe, and structural capital. We were frankly surprised by this finding. There is no overlap between questions that lead to the rating of each component. There is no

Table 8.1 Ranking of IC Management Scores (from high to low)

Rank	Component	Category
1	Management	Human Capital
2	Employees	Human Capital
3	Network	Relationship Capital
4	Customers	Relationship Capital
5	Brand	Relationship Capital
6	Business Recipe	Business Recipe
7	Process	Structural Capital
8	Intellectual Property	Structural Capital

overlap, for example, between employees and management or process and intellectual property (IP). Nevertheless, Table 8.1 shows that the average scores of the components in each category are bunched together; it seems clear that there is an overall strength or weakness that runs through all the components of a category.

The high overall human capital rating may be related to the sample. All the companies in this group chose to undertake an IC assessment, which could be considered a cutting-edge management activity. That may indicate a level of vision and influence of the management team that is translated into the high ratings from the stakeholders. There is also some degree of self-selection. It is unlikely that a management team with serious deficiencies or weak relationship networks would seek to have stakeholders participate in this kind of evaluation. Thus, it is safe to say that the sample includes management teams that are generally confident.

These results do not mean that the companies in the sample are perfect in terms of their human and relationship capital. In fact, there are numerous examples of outlying scores that provoked breakthrough thinking. In the management component of the rating, we often see teams receiving high ratings for their ability to make decisions and communicate externally. But this is often offset by lower ratings related to internal communications, feedback, involvement, and creating an effective culture.

In terms of process, current effectiveness is usually higher than renewal. This often implies that the management team is comfortable with its current success and not worrying as much as they should about the future—we see this pattern for both highly successful companies as well as those facing more significant challenges. Another important pattern frequently seen is organizations pursuing incremental improvements as opposed to more significant innovations that lead to breakthroughs in product development, processes, and/or business recipe.

In branding, high awareness is often offset by low differentiation. And strong customer relationships many times turn out to be with customers who do not provide the profitability and strategic future that the organization seeks.

A Bigger Story

There is a richness to the individual stories of companies in this study. But, pulling back to the overall results, it appears that there is another overarching story. We believe that these rankings tell the story of a search for new business models in the knowledge era. Moving down the list from human to relationship, business recipe, and structural capital corresponds to the journey faced by modern managers from the most to the least familiar concepts and assets in the modern enterprise. As seen in Figure 8.1, the degree of difficulty increases as one moves along the spectrum toward structural capital, including intellectual property.

In general, the work done by employees and managers has changed over time. Today, most workplaces have growing numbers of knowledge workers.

Human ➔ Relationship ➔ Business Recipe ➔ Structural Capital

Figure 8.1 Intangibles Management Degree of Difficulty.

However, the presence of human capital—employees and managers—in the workplace is not a novelty. Although there is surely room for improvement, most companies have processes in place for understanding and managing their workforce. There are new challenges related to the unique nature of knowledge work. However, based on the experience in this sample, it is clear that there are greater challenges in the other categories of IC.

The next category is relationship capital. This, too, has always been a fundamental part of business. Customers, suppliers, financiers, media, and regulators have always been critical to the operation of a business. The knowledge economy has led to new challenges brought on by increased outsourcing and the growing importance of networks, such as the central value of Google's user network to its overall success. Nevertheless, as with human capital, most companies have established ways in place to deal with their network of customers, suppliers, and partners.

But the increased pace of change in markets, technologies, and business models is creating conditions for which many companies are not ready. Competitive position is one of the lowest overall scores for companies in the database. Here, there may also be some influence of self-selection. Most companies that choose to undergo an assessment process have some concerns about the future. The relatively low ranking of business recipe may reflect that these companies are looking for change—and that finding the path to change is not easy.

This leaves us with structural capital. Knowledge and process have always been a part of business. However, in the past, it was usually possible to see, touch, and feel these processes in the form of production lines, design drawings, and delivery networks. Today, most processes occur inside computers, servers, and virtual networks spread across the globe. Discrete processes and pieces of knowledge can be harder to "see."

But it is structural capital that provides the greatest opportunity to your business. The ability to leverage information technology to connect and empower your people (human capital) and your partners (relationship capital) to create repeatable, scalable business processes (structural capital) should be one of the major focuses of the modern manager. It is the opportunity that we hope that we can help you realize through the exercises in the book.

Selected Cases

The second study of the IC Rating user base was presented at the 2009 European Conference on Intellectual Capital. It was based on in-depth interviews of nine managers who had used the tool in their own companies.[6] The lessons shared by these managers included:

- One of the toughest sells in starting an IC assessment is internal. It is advisable to invest time up front introducing the concepts of IC and the goals of the process before it begins.
- Engaging external stakeholders is a very valuable part of the process. There is less resistance from them up front. To make the most of the experience, keep them in the loop afterward and show them how you have taken action on their feedback.
- IC assessment needs to be integrated in the company's strategy process. An assessment should be part of an iterative strategy process that circulates from assessment to strategy, then execution, performance measurement, and back to assessment.
- Key Performance Indicators (KPIs) are an important way of measuring performance of IC. Assessment highlights strengths that can be leveraged and weaknesses that should be improved. Establishing KPIs for the key strategic IC efforts keeps these goals at the forefront and helps the company internalize its understanding of the importance of IC.
- The link between IC and financial results is still hard to establish. None of these early adopters had "cracked the code" to be able to identify the direct link between IC and financials.
- IC is not going away. The move to a knowledge economy continues to accelerate. Understanding the knowledge side of business will be increasingly critical.

This study highlighted the need for the kind of system described in this book that enables companies to link intangible asset performance with financial results.

THE FUTURE OF ASSESSMENTS

In the future, there will be many more assessment tools. But the stakes will also be raised. We believe that assessments will become more and more sophisticated as specific guidelines are developed for the management of knowledge assets. This will be accomplished through the creation of specific processes related to intangibles management.

The study and management of process is already a sophisticated field with international standards in many cases from organizations like the International Organization for Standardization (called "ISO" in English). Over time, processes will be standardized for functions like competency management, process management, and customer relationship management (which you will note represent three of the major components of your knowledge factory).

But will there be an over riding model for all businesses? Eventually, yes. We believe that we will get to a point where there is a generic set of business standards for intangibles management that is applicable across a wide variety of companies and industries. In addition, as with all business studies, there will be norms for intangibles management in particular industries that will emerge.

We would like to see this process speeded up through the creation of an open source set of assessment standards that are available on the Internet and that can be improved over time through community involvement of the companies that use them. We hope that this book will be a starting point and serve as a catalyst for development of a kind of open source intangibles management system.

CONCLUSION

Individual businesses and our economy as a whole currently pay a price for the lack of balance sheets that include the intangible capital assets crucial to corporate success in the knowledge era. Unfortunately, as we have seen in this chapter and the previous one, it may never be possible to replace the balance sheet as it is currently constructed. Therefore, a new approach is needed. The approach outlined here is to create an assessment that taps into the wisdom of stakeholders to evaluate the current capacity, future outlook, and risk of the full knowledge factory. This approach can cut right to the important questions about the knowledge held within an organization's net-work and its ability to exploit it in the future.

The research that we shared showed that companies are generally better at the management of their human and relationship capital. The greater chal-lenge is in the creation and exploitation of structural capital, a serious short-coming because structural capital is the most scalable of the intangible assets.

Assessment is basically a bottom-up form of measurement. It values the opinion of stakeholders to determine the strength and potential of intangi-ble capital. This may sound radical at first. But as you read through to our final chapter on reputation, you will come to see that it is your stakeholders that already set the value of your organization. So the earlier you seek their input, the better off you will be.

EXERCISE

Is your knowledge factory functioning as well as it should?

- Begin with the inventory you made of your knowledge factory in Part I.
- Create questions about each piece of the factory. Ideally ask questions about current status, renewal, and development for the future and areas of risk.
- Identify the stakeholder group that will be surveyed, ranging from the management team to a broad group of internal and external stakeholders.
- Perform the assessment and present the findings to your internal and/or external stakeholders.
- Incorporate the findings into your strategic planning and performance measurement systems.

You can download a worksheet for this exercise at www.intangiblecapitalbook.com.

Performance Measurement Is the New Income Statement

Income Statement
The income statement is the universal scorecard for business. It is the way that a company tracks and communicates its progress month to month and year to year to tell its operating story. The key components are the revenues the company earns by selling goods and services to its customers, the direct costs of those goods, and all the other current year operating costs of the organization. The difference between revenue and cost is profit, often called "the bottom line."

The income statement is still the main tool we have to measure the profitability of an organization. It is the one place that all the financial flows come together—revenues, expenses, and amortization of capital expenditures. But the income statement has been distorted by the rise of the knowledge economy. This has led to the rise of a new kind of reporting of the operating story, called the performance measurement system.

We have already shown how organizations throughout the economy began to invest more heavily in intangibles beginning in the 1970s and 1980s. We saw in the last two chapters how this expense led to a gap between corporate value and the balance sheets because these intangible investments are not eligible to be capitalized. The income statement has also been distorted by the rise of the knowledge economy in two ways.

The first is the understatement of earnings from the inclusion of intangibles investments as operating expenses. The second is the loss of the operating "story" that existed in the industrial era that enabled you to use financial statements to track the entire operating process of a company from the purchase of raw material to the collection of payment for finished goods by your customers.

In this chapter, we talk about both sets of distortions and explain why this has fueled the emergence of a field called performance measurement. We'll explain to you that there are really two approaches to performance measurement out there, what we call *operational* and *managerial*. We'll show you the basics of each kind of performance measurement and show you how to use the exercises in the previous chapters to create your performance measurement system.

UNDERSTATED EARNINGS

The first consequence of the rise of the knowledge economy on the income statement has been that earnings have been understated for the past 30 years by a lot. If you have ever created or used an income statement you probably know the accountants' definition of the income statement is that it contains revenues and expenses related to the current year's operations. Revenues and expenses related to future periods have to be moved off the income statement because they would distort the operating story. Investment in building future value or infrastructure which is expected to be used over more than the current year should be excluded from the income statement. But that's not the way that it has worked with intangibles. And organizations across the United States and across the globe have invested trillions of dollars in intangibles and "paid" for it through their current year earnings.

Of course, this situation is favorable because it lowers taxable income. Further, the cost of building intangibles infrastructure such as process and information technology (IT) is not as concentrated as building a brick-and-mortar factory; it is often built up incrementally over the years. In fact, it is often advisable to spread spending over time to allow the organization to adjust and adapt itself to the changes that the automation of process often require.

There are those who will read this and say it was all for the better. It forced companies to be judicious in their spending and to ensure that they got return on their investment. It saved on taxes. It was the conservative approach to accounting, which would rather err on the side of understating revenue and overstating costs. You may see this picture and say, "We've done OK so far, why shake things up?" Why not leave well enough alone? The truth is that there have been real consequences of this distortion. Earnings that are diminished by intangibles investments put a company that is building for the future at a disadvantage. As you saw in Chapter 7, this creates significant distortions to the public markets.

THE LOST OPERATING STORY

Beyond the distortion of earnings, there has been a second significant prob-lem in the income statement caused by the shift to a knowledge economy. Financials no longer tell the operating story of a company. Most people have gotten used to this fact and don't really think about it. But it is a pretty big deal.

As we explained in Chapter 8, we learned as bankers to trace the full operating cycle of a company from the purchase of raw materials all the way to collection of the accounts receivable. By using simple calculations, we could compare current period revenue and costs (usually on a monthly basis) with different classes of assets to know whether the operations were staying in synch. These calculations included ratios for days of different kinds of inventory on hand, days of receivables and payables—which exam-ined month-to-month and year-to-year told us the operating trends of the company.

Behind the scenes, there was a whole other level of tracking called cost accounting. This was the marriage of accounting and engineering, enabling a manager to understand the cost of each step in a process, the use of overhead by different parts of the production process and other operating units. In sum, the financial system could be used to measure and track almost everything of import going on inside a company. Until the knowledge era came along.

This system falls down when the operations include information flows through and into knowledge assets. Think back to the models we showed you of knowledge factories in Chapter 3. Let's talk about how you account for the functioning of these factories. Sometimes, there is a physical product involved—you already know how to account for that. But even physical products have knowledge components. And knowledge flows in companies are much harder to track. The use of a process does not lower the "inven-tory" of knowledge contained in the process. In fact, as we have seen, use of knowledge can increase the knowledge by adapting to lessons learned during use. You can allocate the cost of human capital to the work they are doing. But you cannot account for the "use" of a relationship because it is not a financial asset. To tell the operating story of the knowledge factory, you need to move beyond financial measures.

NONFINANCIAL INDICATORS

The lack of a clear operating story in the financials means that it is impor-tant to find nonfinancial indicators to enable an organization to track the progression of its work. The use of nonfinancial measurement is not new. Factories in the industrial era were not managed using just financial data. There were other kinds of metrics that were used to monitor the function-ing of each production line and the factory as a whole. Examples include the output of the production line each hour, the number of defects per thousand products, and the amount of scrap generated. This kind of mea-surement was facilitated by gauges and dials on production equipment, spot counts for quality control, and measuring the scrap hauled away from the line. Over the course of the last century, industrial companies developed more and more sophisticated ways of measuring, managing, and optimizing production of physical goods.

To optimize your knowledge production, you also have many options for nonfinancial indicators. We will just give you a taste of common indicators for each of the categories of intangible capital (IC). You will recognize some of them as the "demographic" data that we suggested for use in combination with intangible capital expenditure figures in Chapter 7.

Human Capital:
- Number of full-time, part-time, and contract employees
- Education level of employees
- Training/certifications of employees
- Average tenure and/or turnover of employees

Relationship Capital:
- For each key relationship type (customers, vendors, partners): Size of relationship, length of relationship, relationship trend
- Number of industry verticals, relationship distributions within those verticals
- Number of brands

Structural Capital:
- Process performance (speed, volume, service levels)
- Intellectual property (IP) portfolio (number of patents, grouping by areas of expertise or knowledge families, number of licenses)

These indicators provide the most basic parameters for intangible capital. Depending on the nature of your business, there are hundreds of other indicators that you may decide to track. For example, communication patterns among knowledge workers can be tracked—by counting the number of e-mails, phone calls, instant messages, and face-to-face conversations of each employee—to help optimize communication practices. Knowledge can be tracked—by recording detailed profiles of each employee's skills, experience, and networks—to facilitate team formation. Or projects can be tracked as they move through the stages of a project management system—to improve the process as well as the content of your employees' work.

The most important question for any manager is: what is the right set of indicators that is appropriate for your business? This is the core question you must face as you build your own performance measurement system.

HOW TO BUILD YOUR OWN PERFORMANCE MEASUREMENT SYSTEM

We believe that the major reason for the rise of performance measurement as a discipline is the rise of the knowledge economy. Performance measurement is a way of coping with the broken accounting paradigm. And it is a reflection of good management by providing a perspective that is proactive, focusing on the factors that will lead to the financial results that a company wants to achieve. But this book is a rebuttal to anyone who believes that you can rely on a performance measurement system alone to help you cope with the shift to the knowledge era.

Today, performance measurement is much more common than the tracking of intangible capital expenditure and the assessment of intangible capital that we outlined in the previous two chapters. We view this as a huge shortcoming of existing approaches to intangibles management.

Your goal should be to develop a deep enough understanding of your organization, particularly its knowledge factory, and to be able to find the best, most innovative ways of leveraging your knowledge for its highest and best use—and greatest profit. So, if you haven't read the book up to this point, consider turning back. Because a performance measurement system should be built on a sound set of basic information about your company, not just indicators.

START AT THE BEGINNING

The knowledge factory is the way that you create value, convert your knowledge into usable (and hopefully scalable) forms, and get paid. Just as you would with a tangible factory, there are basic management activities that need to be associated with the knowledge factory. The management information set for the knowledge factory should follow this sequence. You will notice that this sequence corresponds to the material you have read thus far in this book:

1. *Inventory*—As explained in Part I, the first step to understanding the knowledge side of your business is to take an inventory of the competencies, relationships, brands, processes, and intellectual property to which you have access. Identify your business recipe and model the business to show how you combine your unique IC to create value for your customers and get paid. Update this list at least annually.

2. *Investment*—As recommended in Chapter 7, it makes a lot of sense to keep track of how much you are investing in the intangibles on your inventory. Knowing these numbers will help your management team and board make better decisions. It will also help other stakeholders understand your priorities. Over time, you will be able to use the data to learn more about the effectiveness of your investments. Set up your chart of accounts so that intangibles investments are easy to identify and generate a report on a quarterly or annual basis.

3. *Assessment*—Chapter 8 explains how to evaluate each of the intangibles on your inventory. Are they adequate for today's needs? What about future needs? Where are you at risk?

4. *Strategy*—Armed with an understanding of your key intangibles and how they fit in your business model, you can make better decisions about what your priorities need to be for the coming year for your deliberate and emergent strategies.

5. *Performance Measurement*—Then you can design a performance measurement system, as we describe in this chapter. This kind of metric is monitored on an ongoing basis or at least monthly.
6. *Financial Results*—Ultimately, your intangible assets and knowledge factory will lead to financial results (if they don't, go back to Chapter 1 and look at the sections on monetizing intangibles).
7. *Start Again at the Beginning*—Management information should be a way to learn and improve your operations. Ideally, you will have a continuous flow of a variety of information types and enough flexibility built into your system to allow for adaptation over time.

Over time, you will see the value of each of the kinds of measurement sources we have talked about thus far: investment, assessment, and indicators. There is a lot of potential for learning by comparing the three kinds of data points to triangulate an understanding of your knowledge assets, a concept we discuss more at the end of this chapter.

Building a performance measurement system without the right foundation information would be like designing a dashboard when you have never looked under the hood of a car. "Now, wait a minute," you will say, "I know my business inside and out." And you probably do. But no matter how deep your personal familiarity with the business, it still makes sense to build systems that can provide the right kind of information and controls to keep it on track. This is true in every size company. Knowledge that is concentrated in the head of an individual is knowledge that is at risk. A good performance measurement system is an essential part of the structural capital supporting your organization.

We once had a client that had close to several million dollars of inventory in their warehouse. It was a service business and they used the products in the warehouse in client installations. And, believe it or not, they didn't have an inventory system. Project managers would order materials under a job system so the cost got billed to the client. But the physical movement was tracked in people's heads. The materials would show up. The warehouse manager would do his best to figure out what came in and which job it belonged to. But, it may not surprise you that they often lost materials and ended up double-ordering, often paying express shipping rates to get the product in by the installation date. Sounds pretty dysfunctional, doesn't it?

These people knew their business in and out. It honestly took them a long time to understand that there would be a significant return on the relatively low cost of developing an inventory system. You are probably thinking, "That's not us. We would never do something that silly." Then we only have one question: Have you completed the inventory of your knowledge factory yet?

With good information, you will learn over time how much investment, for example, is needed to keep the quality and outlook of an intangible strong, how that intangible affects your overall profitability, and how its performance can be measured in the interim using indicators. This kind of holistic approach is still in its infancy. The starting point is to gather good data. As you do this, however, you need to understand the implication of your intent on the kind of data you get and the actions that result from your measurement process.

THE IMPORTANCE OF INTENT

The reason behind your measurement, your intent, can actually end up influencing what happens in the measured activity. We call the two basic intents or perspectives of measurement systems managerial and operational. This distinction is actually another facet of the story that we have already cited about the tension in the modern organization between the bottom up and the top down.

This idea crystallized for us a few years ago when we read Ian Graham's article, "What's Wrong with Targets?" Graham made the case that setting targets or goals for employees creates the wrong kind of behavior. This is because it focuses the employee on the target rather than on the underlying processes that create value for customers and stakeholders. And once a goal is achieved, there is often no reason to reach further. He also asserts that targets can be gamed. The alternative he suggests is to focus on specific processes and measure everything you can with an eye to continuous learning. His perspective comes out of the quality movement and the concept of continuous improvement.[1]

We thought of Graham recently when we read an article about the games that colleges play to ensure that they meet the thresholds for statistics used by US News and others to "rank" colleges. Areas that can be manipulated include soliciting alumni donations of as little as $1 to increase their alumni giving percentage, giving more weight to applicant GPA and SAT scores than in the past, and manipulating class size.[2] Anyone who has ever worked in a for-profit or not-for-profit organization knows that goals can drive behavior in good and bad ways.

We were so intrigued by this contrarian view of targets and goals that Mary actually led a program at the Institute of Management Consultants to discuss it. We have also broached the subject with a number of our clients. Most people agree that goals should drive learning. But there is also near unanimity on the fact that it is actually often necessary to set targets to spark employees' imaginations, to help them understand the organization's direction, and to create incentives for success. Most businesspeople find it hard to imagine an organization without goals and targets.

One of the big reasons that goals are so important in many organizations is the fact that compensation is tied to an employee's ability to reach a goal. Daniel Pink's new book, Drive: The Surprising Truth About What Really Motivates Us, documents scientific evidence that compensation for knowledge work based on goals is actually counter productive. A clear monetary reward works well in situations where the task to be performed is understood and well-defined. In contrast, incentives are counter productive for problem-solving tasks (which includes the work of most knowledge workers)—leading the person to underperform.[3] Pink is respected for his work to date on the knowledge economy (*Free Agent Nation* and *A Whole New Mind*). It will be interesting to see if he can take on the ideology of incentives that is so deeply ingrained in American business.

You are probably like most businesspeople and cannot imagine a world without goals. But please at least take the time to understand the difference between the operational and the managerial perspectives—and think about what it means for your business.

Operational Metrics:

Bottom-up, using lots of data with a focus on:
- Learning
- Continuous improvement
- Quality

Managerial Metrics:

Top-down, using key performance indicators with a focus on:
- Communicating strategy
- Creating incentives for performance
- External communication

Operations-Oriented Measurement

Operations measurement is the use of nonfinancial indicators to track the work that is being done in your organization. This kind of measurement is an open process focused on measuring as many things as can be measured. We view this as a bottom-up process. The reason that we describe operational measurement as bottom-up is that it is so similar to many of the Web 2.0 bottom-up trends—you don't know what is going to come out of it, you cannot control it, but you will learn from it. That is the spirit of operational measurement: trying to measure as much as you can and using it to get better, smarter, and faster. The spirit of it is learning.

This approach got a lot of attention in *Numerati* by Stephen Baker. Baker shows us the extraordinary potential of large pools of data for learning (for good and sometimes for harm, depending on your perspective). The book covers a broad range of data that are/will be mined across our society and markets with chapters dedicated to data on shopping, voting, medicine, and working. The depth of analysis outlined by Baker is the logical outgrowth of the amount of data now available along with tools to begin to make sense of it all. If your organization is in a position to create robust measurement systems, then we absolutely encourage you to do so, with the proviso we discuss below about not relying exclusively on performance measurement and ignoring the investment and assessment approaches that were the focus of the last two chapters.

Measuring everything that can be measured is an overly optimistic goal for many organizations. We know from experience that many important things are still not measured at all in some organizations. We have seen this problem in companies of all sizes. We worked with a large company that had huge differences in the financial performance of different partnerships yet they had never developed a data set to try to figure out the critical differences between high and low performers.

So we recommend getting the basics right first. And we do not want to encourage you to take on more than you can handle. But the truth is that you should be able to track all of your core processes, all the components of your knowledge factory. The key is to think about the critical path of the process, and the metrics that will help you see whether it is functioning as it should.

Management-Oriented Measurement

Targets and goals are top-down metrics that are used for control and reporting purposes. They are used to signal important business drivers, to create incentives for meeting the targets, and to track performance against a strategy. We call these *managerial metrics*. The users of this information are usually in a managerial and/or finance function. They tend to have more of a bias toward using metrics as a score of success or failure. As mentioned above, employee evaluations and compensation are often tied to this kind of metric. As such they become a way of setting and creating incentives to reach certain goals. Learning does not always get the attention it should in this approach.

The rise of the management branch of performance measurement is being fueled by a number of trends. One is the emergence of software that helps companies automate the creation of dashboards that have live feeds of the critical information that will tell a management team how well its operation is performing. These software vendors as well as many management consultants and academics advocate the identification and tracking of key performance indicators (KPIs) which are the small number of leading indicators of the organization's progress toward its goals.

Chief in this camp, although by no means alone, is the Balanced Scorecard (BSC) system laid out in a series of books by Robert S. Kaplan and David P. Norton. The BSC has been one of the main ways that companies (especially in the United States) have attempted to fill the intangibles information gap. The growth in this field has been fueled by a U.S. business culture that values hard data and tangible results. It feels good to managers trained in the ways of the industrial era (which includes almost everyone reading this book) to be able to talk about the key drivers of performance in their company and demonstrate that they can generate verifiable data to back it up.

The starting point for the BSC is the organization's strategy, where they want to go. Then the path to the ultimate financial goals is drawn using a "strategy map" which connects financial goals with nonfinancial perspectives. This is primarily a top-down exercise that Kaplan and Norton actually recommend be managed by an Office of Strategic Management.

The perspectives used in the BSC correspond roughly—although not completely—to the categories of intangible capital.[4] The following shows Kaplan and Norton's category with the IC category to which it belongs in parentheses:

- Learning and growth (a subset of human capital)
- Internal business processes (a subset of structural capital)
- Customer (a subset of relationship capital)
- Financial (a subset of business recipe)

Once you get used to the vocabulary of the knowledge factory, it will seem limiting to be confined to learning, process, customers, and financial. Learning ignores the richness of the experience, knowledge, culture, and competencies that employees and managers contribute to human capital. Internal business processes ignores the other forms of captured knowledge and the organization's intellectual property. Customers are a critical relationship for every company but, as you have seen in earlier chapters, customers are far from being the only external relationships in today's interconnected world where suppliers and partners become a critical part of the operational network. Finally, although financial results remain the critical metric for companies, there are other important parts of the business recipe which should be considered.

We are not trying to discourage you from developing a balanced scorecard. On the contrary, it is very important to develop a scorecard of some sort as a replacement for the operational information you used to get from your accounting department. We are just trying to encourage you to broaden your horizons by including your entire knowledge factory—your full intangible capital portfolio.

Further, while we know that you will probably feel the need to use goals and targets in your own organization, we also hope that you will also use measurement and indicators for learning. There is room for both approaches and, in the long run, each perspective can enhance the value of the other.

BEWARE MAGIC METRICS

We have another word of warning for you: It is never a good idea to rely exclusively on a small number of indicators. This warning is necessary because business publications are full of articles about what we call magic metrics. They offer an easy solution that will seemingly solve all your problems. The following are just a few examples.

A classic case comes from customer call centers. For a long time, companies like Dell used to track the length of each call into their call centers. This seemed like a good way to measure the work being done. However, this measurement ended up putting a lot of pressure on customer service representatives to get a call over with. And it did nothing to solve the customer's problem. Now Dell and others track the number of problems resolved, minutes to resolution, and number of calls to reach resolution.[5]

In the past few years, McKinsey has been producing really interesting data about the revenue and profit per employee at leading companies. It shows big differences between specific companies which led to the conclusion that "thinking-intensive workers" could return much greater financial results to their employers. Microsoft and Cisco were at the top while Intel, Johnson & Johnson, and GE were all in the middle of the pack.[6] This was really interesting and informative as historical data. But we have also seen people promoting profit per employee as a KPI which could be very dangerous. This number can be easily gamed through layoffs or outsourcing of personnel which would improve the ratio but may hurt the company in the long run.

Another metric getting a lot of attention is the Net Promoter Score (NPS). A customer who is a "promoter" is thought to be likely to recommend a company to friends and/or colleagues. Research from Bain identified a link between high NPS and corporate growth.[7] But subsequent research showed that it wasn't the magic bullet that it appeared to be.[8] Does this mean that it is a bad metric? No, it's just not the only metric that a company should use. A quick note, if you are paying attention, you will notice that this is actually not an indicator but, rather, an assessment based on customer surveys. But the message is the same—don't put too much faith in small numbers of data points.

In your own business, there will always be KPIs that everyone accepts as the right measures for your business. They may be. But never run your business with just one number and always try to find new indicators that match what you are trying to accomplish. It is important to the success of your business. And the ante will be upped when you have to talk to your external stakeholders about your KPIs—which you will, as we explain in the next chapter.

TRIANGULATION

Once you have a full set of data about your intangibles, how should you use it? We like to use the image of triangulation seen in Figure 9.1 as a way of explaining how you can use the three kinds of data that we have described to come up with a unified measurement of your intangibles. Triangulation is an approach used in a number of disciplines (including surveying and astronomy) using known points to plot out an unknown distance or space. With intangibles, you can use these three kinds of data— investment, assessment, and indicators—to plot out the landscape of your intangibles and get comfortable with the future earnings potential of your business.

In this drawing, the starting point is the investment calculation for intangibles. Since it is a financial measurement, we show it intersecting with the calculation of earnings potential. But assessment and indicators are nonfinancial metrics. They shed light on the capacity of the intangibles through analysis (assessment) and direct measurement (indicators). That's why they

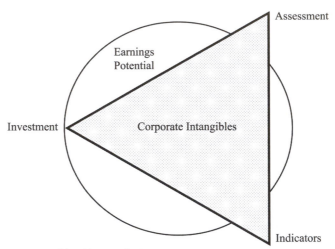

Figure 9.1 Intangibles Triangulation.

are shown as defining a different shape, although it is one that overlaps with the earnings potential. Triangulation of intangibles does not add up to an auditable number. But it does shed light on the critical intangible sources of value and future earnings potential of a company. And these measures provide much richer and more accurate information than the gut feel of a manager or an analyst that is in use today.

The exact measurement of intangibles is still in its infancy. Over time, our collective skills in this kind of analysis will improve. But if you use investment, assessment, and indicators, you will be able to triangulate, to come up with an understanding of the health and workings of your organization's intangibles. Most reporting solutions, in fact, use a combination of these metrics to help create a data set about intangibles.

NEW REPORTING SYSTEMS

To give you an idea of how this kind of approach can work in practice, we profile three projects. The first is an approach developed by the PwC Corporate Reporting Group. It is a Value Analysis Statement that combines several measurement approaches. The left-hand column includes 21 value-creating activities divided into six categories of value: innovation, brand, customer, human capital, supply chain, and environmental/social. Then for each category, various data columns report:[9]

- Historic cash flow from that activity
- Prospective cash flow indicators (an arrow up, level, or down)
- Risk indicators (names the risks but does not measure)
- Nonfinancial indicators
- Historic trends for the nonfinancial indicators
- Objective for the nonfinancial indicators going forward

This is a sound approach from PwC that combines the several kinds of intangibles data—investment, assessment, and indicators—with financial results to give a richer picture of the drivers behind the numbers.

The second is a project that began in 2009. It is a reporting approach that is being developed by the Warsaw Stock Exchange for its listed companies. The project is being led by one of our colleague companies in the IC Rating network, Innovatika. We are happy to say that we had a small role in the thinking behind the project, including the need to track intangibles investment. The project is in full-scale launch as this book goes to print but we promise to provide updates through our blogs, the IC Knowledge Center, and the book's Web site.

The project has developed two main tools. The first is a management self-assessment that measures the effectiveness, development, and risk vis-à-vis the strategic goals of the company. This tool is for internal use only. The second tool is built on indicators related to the business model, relationship, human, and structural capital. The indicators track investment, the process of turning investments into results, and the results themselves. These indicators are both financial and nonfinancial but are all auditable and used for disclosure to investors and the general market.

The third project is also still in process. This is a reporting product that we are developing jointly with several partners. The tool will be used to help private business owners understand the current and potential value of their businesses. It uses an assessment by stakeholders that compares a company's intangibles with those of its market peers. This helps identify the proper valuation range of the company based on market comparables. There will also be a related tool that will help the company create a set of financial and nonfinancial indicators to track its progress against improvement plans for critical value drivers.

BARRIERS TO CHANGE

When you think about it, it's incredible that the intangible information gap still exists. American business culture is supremely focused on getting hard data to make decisions. Yet the business community continues to turn a blind eye to the fact that they lack information on the lion's share of their corporate value and success. Yes, a good manager has an intuitive feel for the intangible drivers of his or her business. But, if you asked them or their stakeholders whether a business should rely primarily on intuition, they would laugh you out of the board room. Most people are in a state of denial. Why? We think there are two reasons.

First, no one is asking management teams for this information. Remember that the investment community, corporate managers, boards of directors, bankers, accountants, and even regulators all studied in the same schools. They read the same business publications. They all lack the background to ask the right questions and to get accurate answers. So no one asks and no one answers.

Second, as so often happens with change, people think they have a vested interest in the status quo. For example, if you ask an analyst or investor, they will tell you that they already follow intangibles. They spend a lot of time reading about the company and speaking to management to identify the critical value drivers and "get behind the numbers" to supplement their own understanding of the company's results. They are right to a degree. In fact, analysts and investors often develop their own analytical models as a way to make sense of company and industry results. Many are very fond of their way of looking at the world and feel that their analytical approaches represent personal intangible capital, their own unique value, which gives them a leg up on their own competitors. Why would they seek more transparency?

You could say that managers as a group have a particularly strong vested interest in the current system. The importance of a manager increases in situations where there is poor information. In these cases, the manager becomes a critical information source. In fact, communication of information (both up and down the organization) was an important role of managers in the industrial model. Seeking more transparency may diminish this traditional role although, as we made the case in Chapter 5, there is still plenty for managers to do in the knowledge enterprise.

These barriers are not insurmountable. However, they do exist. And any successful effort to change the status quo must address them directly. You could say that this book is an effort to address these barriers. The lack of understanding of intangibles holds back all the stakeholders in our financial system. We hope that improved understanding will lead investors, boards, managers, and stakeholders of all kinds to start asking the right questions.

CONCLUSION

Performance measurement is probably the most common approach to intangibles measurement in today's market. These systems are usually built for managerial as opposed to operational measurement. The managerial approach helps identify key performance indicators that can be used to frame goals and incentives internally. We will see in the next chapter that KPIs are often also used to report on results externally.

The managerial approach can be dangerous when the KPIs are developed without disciplined analysis of investment and assessment approaches described in the previous two chapters. It also overlooks the incredible potential of broader measurement of intangibles for learning and continuous improvement. Find room for both the managerial and operational perspectives in developing your performance measurement system. And don't forget to use more than just indicators. Triangulate the performance of your knowledge factory using all three kinds of intangibles measurements: investment, assessment, and indicators.

EXERCISE

What can/should be measured in your knowledge factory?

- Based on the ratings of the organization's intangible assets, are there changes that should be made to your strategy?
- How would you measure the success of these changes?
- How would you measure the success of your overall strategy (operational measures for learning)?
- What are the KPIs for your overall business (managerial measures for control)?
- Should you communicate your KPIs to key stakeholder groups? Which ones?

You can download a worksheet for this exercise at www.intangiblecapitalbook.com.

Reputation Is the New Bottom Line

The Bottom Line
In both the tangible and the intangible economy, the ultimate metric for all companies is and will be their ability to generate profits—a strong bottom line. Profits and the cash they provide ensure an organization's survival.

In the knowledge economy, it is no longer enough to just produce a strong bottom line. It may sound a little bold to "replace" the most important metric of business success—profits and cash—with an intangible like reputation. Before you panic and skip this chapter, remember that we are both former bankers. We are huge believers in financial success. We are not trying to get you to change your mind about the financial bottom line. It is as important as ever. But, as you must have figured out by now, the knowledge era has made business more complicated. The financial bottom line still tells you whether or not your company made money, but that's about all. As we have explained in detail in the previous chapters, financials do not report on the intangible production capacity of your business. They don't capture the operating story as you invest in, operate, and monetize your intangible capital through your knowledge factory. And, most importantly for your reputation, very little concrete information on intangibles gets through to your stakeholders.

This lack of good information on intangibles means that for many external partners, your business is a black box. They cannot see inside the black box but will assume it is working well as long as you are making money. When something goes wrong, however, and word gets out, they assume that there is probably more bad news on the way. Your stock price will go down. Your partners will start to worry. Job candidates will think twice about joining you. Existing employees doubt the wisdom of sticking around. Even an isolated problem can quickly damage your overall reputation.

The focus on reputation is also being fueled by a second large-scale trend. There is increased pressure on businesses to not only make money but also to be good citizens of the world. This means that the metrics by which you are measured are changing. Add this to the intangibles information gap, and you have a pretty confusing environment for the average businessperson. To date, most companies are hanging tight, figuring that it is better to not say anything than to say the wrong thing. But your stakeholders are going to make up their minds about you anyway. Wouldn't you be better off to help them make the best possible decision?

This chapter defines reputation and explains why it has taken on such great importance in the knowledge era. We help you identify key stakeholders and think about how to manage the reputation that they create for you through better reporting and increased transparency. We will also share research that has been done that shows how this kind of transparency can have a direct effect on your reputation and corporate valuation—and try to motivate you to take advantage of this benefit by dipping your toe into intangibles reporting.

Corporate reporting is still extraordinarily weak when it comes to intangibles. We will make some suggestions on how to improve corporate reporting. We believe there is no question about whether the reporting of intangibles will improve, just a question as to when it will change and what will be the catalyst. No matter what, you can rest assured that in just a matter of years, you will be disclosing information about your intangibles that you did not disclose in the past—and actually benefit from this process by getting a better deal from your bankers, a fairer evaluation from analysts, and a better valuation from investors and merger partners. We'll prepare you for this trend—and maybe convince you to become a trendsetter.

THE BOTTOM LINE AND SHAREHOLDER VALUE

U.S. business culture is very much about results. Two of the ideas that best capture this perspective are the concepts of the bottom line and shareholder value. The bottom line is a financial calculation. As we have made clear throughout this book, the integrity of financial statements that are used to calculate the profit or loss of an enterprise is seriously compromised by their failure to address knowledge intangibles. Profit and cash flow are still important to the day-to-day survival of a business. But focusing on today's bottom line without regard to tomorrow's bottom line can lead you to make bad decisions: to outsource a function that should be a core competency; to fail to invest in an intangible that will preserve and protect a competitive advantage. Peter Drucker put it this way, "Our traditional mind-set . . . has always somehow perceived business as buying cheap and selling dear. The new approach defines a business as the organization that adds value and creates wealth."[1]

The question of value has actually been at the forefront of American business vocabulary for several decades. The "maximization of shareholder value" is a core doctrine that has rarely been subject to much question. Who could argue? It seems to be the most sensible idea there is; a corporation must measure itself by the value it builds for its shareholders. The problem has come in how this idea has been applied. The metric used for evaluating a public company's shareholder value is its stock price. Again, seemingly simple on the surface. But stock prices move minute-to-minute and day-to-day. This is an even shorter-term measure than last year's bottom line. Yet it is regularly used as a justification for strategic decisions, not to mention employee compensation schemes. Seen this way, the concept of shareholder value and the bottom line have been at the root of a lot of dangerous short-term thinking.

Many associate Jack Welch, former CEO of GE, with this concept, citing a speech Welch gave in 1981 entitled, "Growing Fast in a Slow-Growth Economy." But in March 2009 he denied that he ever intended to send a message that share price should be of paramount importance. He told the *Financial Times* that, "The idea that shareholder value is a strategy is insane. . . . Shareholder value is a result, not a strategy. . . . Your main constituencies are your employees, your customers, and your products."[2]

Then in September 2009, the Aspen Institute released a paper signed by a group of 28 executives that included Warren Buffet (CEO, Berkshire Hathaway), Lou Gerstner (Retired CEO, IBM), and John Bogle (Founder, The Vanguard Group). The paper, entitled "Overcoming Short-Termism," opens by saying:

> In recent years, boards, managers, shareholders with varying agendas and regulators, all, to one degree or another, have allowed short-term considerations to overwhelm the desirable long-term growth and sustainable profit objectives of the corporation. . . . We believe that short-term objectives have eroded faith in corporations. . . . Restoring that faith critically requires restoring a long-term focus . . . if not voluntarily, then by appropriate regulation.[3]

There are those who believe that in the long term, shareholders themselves will force a move away from a short-term perspective. The majority of public stock in the United States and the United Kingdom is now owned by small investors or by pension and investment plans whose money comes from everyday citizens. In *The New Capitalists: How Citizen Investors Are Reshaping the Corporate Agenda*, Stephen Davis, Jon Lukomnik, and David Pitt-Watson make the case that this change in ownership will drive increased corporate activism. These "citizen investors" are beginning to realize that they have a voice. And the voice is not focused on one company or another maximizing profits to the detriment of the economy as a whole. This voice is concerned with profits but also with long-term value creation and responsible corporate citizenship.

AN EXPANDED VIEW OF RELATIONSHIP CAPITAL

This discussion means that we have to now expand the definition of relationship capital used in the rest of our book. The primary focus of this book has been on understanding and managing your knowledge factory, the intangible capital system by which you create value for your customers. The primary relationship capital of the knowledge factory includes your customers, partners, and vendors. We have also focused on the human capital, especially in terms of the competencies that your people bring to the knowledge factory.

In thinking about reputation, however, it is important to flip the perspective and see your company through the eyes of your people and your partners. As contributors to the knowledge factory, they are also stakeholders in its success. What do they think of the organization? Does it seem sustainable? Is it a place they want to be or to do business with?

There are countless factors influencing that judgment by your employees and stakeholders. For your employees, it's about being a good place to work, about compensation and growth. For your customers, it's about your product, your service, your pricing, and how you stand up against the competition. For both, it's about the quality of your structural capital, the amount of collective knowledge in your system, and using what you know to create value. Increasingly, it's also about how you behave as a corporate citizen. Your environmental footprint, your social contributions, your fairness, and transparency. The perspective that's important here is the perspective of the employee and the stakeholder. It's about what they think, not what you think. And whether what they think is enough of an incentive to stay connected to you.

There are also new categories of relationship capital that must be mentioned. These include stakeholders such as investors, bankers, neighbors, markets, and even society as a whole. Investors are interested in your financial results and your capacity to continue to produce results in the future. Bankers have a direct interest in the continuing success and viability of your business. Neighbors include the communities that live and work near your facilities or are affected by your product or services. Markets include your competitors and participants in markets related to yours. Society as a whole includes stakeholders that are interested in legal, environmental, and systemic consequences of your organization's actions. Each of these has varied interests. And any one of them can withdraw their support if they believe their interests are not being served.

What holds the whole thing together? Your reputation. Being a good (or good enough) employer. Being a good (or good enough) partner. Your stakeholders collectively create your reputation and they will make their stay-or-leave decisions based on that same reputation. That means that your reputation is your license to earn money in the future. Last year's earnings tell you the financial bottom line but they don't tell you whether you are in a good position for a repeat performance. For this, reputation is a much stronger indicator. As the sum total of your company's value, your reputation will be set through the consensus of your stakeholders.

WHY NOW?

If you are reading critically, you are probably thinking, "Wait a minute. What's different now? Companies have always had employees and customers. They've never owned them. Why do they have more influence now?" There are actually several forces driving this change.

You have already heard about the first driver, the shift in the control of the means of production. In the industrial era, a company's profits were driven by what it owned. Workers had to come to the employer to get access to the means of production. It gave companies a greater level of control over its workers. With the rise of the knowledge economy, however, the knowledge held by employees and, indeed, external stakeholders has become an important part of a corporation's "means of production." The knowledge factory relies on the unique contribution of human and relationship capital elements. This shift in the balance of power means that companies have to pay more attention to the interests and priorities of their stakeholders as "partners" in the success of the knowledge factory.

The second driver of the increased focus on reputation is the acceleration of communications. In this book, you have already gotten a sense of the growing influence of new Internet-enabled media including blogs, Twitter, and social networks. These are just the latest developments in a society that had already developed 24-hour news. It is easier than ever before for anyone to get a message out. Sometimes all it takes is a blog post or a YouTube video by one disgruntled customer to go viral and threaten your reputation in an instant.

The third driver, we believe, is the lack of transparency of intangibles. We have tried to make the case throughout this book that there is a shocking lack of information available to internal and external stakeholders about the knowledge side of business. So when news does get out about a problem or a failure, then the reaction is swift and often very negative. If you don't understand how a business works and don't receive periodic information beyond just the financials, then bad news is a warning to get out. The less your stakeholders understand about your business and the less you share about the nonfinancial aspects of it, the more vulnerable you are to severe reactions to bad financial news.

The final driver of the focus on reputation is an increased interest in sustainability and corporate social responsibility (often just the acronym CSR is used). This trend reflects growing interest among a variety of stakeholder groups for corporations to take responsibility for more than just their own profits.

SUSTAINABILITY

CFO magazine defines sustainability as:

> The practice of publicizing a company's environmental and social risks, responsibilities and opportunities . . . it can be thought of as an

environmental-impact statement for the entire corporation, with "environment" defined not only in terms of natural resources and climatological effects but also the economic and social impacts of labor practices, charitable endeavors and governance structures.[4]

The need for attention to a broader set of priorities is driven by the same kind of intangible reporting problems that we have described throughout this book. In the industrial economy, overall success of a society was measured by growth in financial metrics like gross national product and rising income levels. No attempt was made to measure nonfinancial gains or losses. This focus on financial metrics means that economists count the sale of oil as productive but do not count its carbon impact. We count food production and sales but not the environmental impact of energy-dependent industrial farming and not the health impact of the kinds of food produced by this system. We count spending on health care but not the health of our population. We count spending on education but not the results of the system. You get the picture.

Many feel it's time to move beyond just the financial profits of individual companies. There are a number of international organizations leading the way in identifying new ways of enhancing financial reporting with information about the nonfinancial effects of corporate behavior. This is sometimes also called the "triple bottom line," for the combination of profits, people, and planet. The United Nations Global Compact[5] espouses 10 principles that explain the scope of this perspective:

Human rights
1. Businesses should support and respect the protection of internationally proclaimed human rights; and
2. Businesses should make sure that they are not complicit in human rights abuses.

Labour
3. Businesses should uphold the freedom of association and the effective recognition of the right to collective bargaining;
4. the elimination of all forms of forced and compulsory labour;
5. the effective abolition of child labour; and
6. the elimination of discrimination in respect of employment and occupation.

Environment
7. Businesses are asked to support a precautionary approach to environmental challenges;
8. undertake initiatives to promote greater environmental responsibility; and
9. encourage the development and diffusion of environmentally friendly technologies.

Anti-corruption
10. Businesses should work against corruption in all its forms, including extortion and bribery.

The framework of the Global Reporting Initiative (GRI) has a similar approach using six families of indicators: economic, environment, human rights, labor, product responsibility, and society. GRI provides detailed guidelines through an open Web site: www.globalreporting.com. To date, 1,200 companies have begun using their standards, half of which are in Europe. Only 10 percent of those using the standards are in the United States. Although this is not an immediate requirement for public companies, it is a growing area of emphasis and one that cannot be ignored in the broader discussion of corporate reputation.

Rules for managing corporate reputation

1. Do things right
2. Be proactive
3. Be transparent

HOW TO MANAGE REPUTATION

It is actually interesting and somewhat perplexing to us that sustainability reporting has received more attention to date than intangibles reporting. The reason this book has a chapter on reputation is that we feel that intangibles management is a key determinant of corporate reputation. The current lack of information available to stakeholders about intangibles puts corporate reputation at increasing risk. When there is incomplete information about the details of business, reputation becomes a proxy for its overall success. That's how small problems can have a much greater effect than perhaps they should. If stakeholders do not have a clear picture of what's going on, they will assume the worst. In the long run, we believe that good intangibles management and transparent communication will diminish the wild swings of reputation that many companies experience today. In the short run, you can make this happen yourself.

Do Things Right

It may sound overly simplistic to say it but the principal way that you should manage your reputation is by getting everything else right. That is the essence of the challenge. Reputation is influenced by what you do, how you do it, and what you say about it. The best defense is to do it all as well as possible. What's the best way to do that? Glad you asked. The answer is to build structural capital.

In Part I of this book, you (hopefully) learned that structural capital is a great way to get rich. Good structural capital takes knowledge and turns it into repeatable, scalable processes that have a low marginal cost. Google's search engine is the best example there is of this kind of structural capital, with $22 billion in revenue and counting. But there is another advantage to structural capital: it enshrines "best practices" of your organization in reusable form. There are different levels of structural capital, with varying degrees of power and benefit. As we look at these levels, you will see a repeat of a number of concepts from earlier parts of the book.

If you take what you know and record it, you will have a set of policies. Policies are good because they create a standard by which work can be done. They also provide a tool by which work can be audited. And hopefully then you will have a set of data that can be used to measure the success of the policy.

Although policies are good, processes are better. Processes are work patterns that are used over and over again in an organization. They are the operationalization of policies. They put policies to work. The best kind of process is automated. It is integrated with the everyday work of the organization. If it is implemented correctly, this ensures that the policy is also followed. All the time.

The best processes of all are those that are audited. A lot of intangibles management should be incorporated into internal reviews of processes and controls. This ensures that learning will happen over time. And, of course, there is always the command and control aspect. Audits are a good way to enforce standards—people are much more likely to do something if they know that someone is watching.

The problems in global supply chains described in Chapter 2 have been the source of a number of reputational crises in recent memory: lead paint used on toys supplied to Mattel; tainted peanut butter supplied to Kellogg for crackers; contaminated milk in China. These kinds of mistakes obviously indicate a problem somewhere between the policy, the process, and the audit. They become reputational crises because they cause sickness and/or endanger the health of large numbers of people.

But the size of the crisis really depends on whether or not the company can pinpoint the problem. The important facts are what happened, how it happened, and what the company is doing to ensure that it will not happen again. The size of the crisis grows depending on which of these three questions you can answer. If you are facing a problem, what happened is already obvious. But can you explain—in light of the policy, process, and audits that you surely have—how it happened? That will diminish the crisis somewhat. But the most important thing you can do is explain how you have changed your policy, process, and audit so it doesn't happen again. Can you answer these questions?

Seen this way, reputation truly is the bottom line for the quality of your operations, your knowledge factory. Good process and quality control are your best insurance policies for continued reputational success. The quality movement has already moved into more and more knowledge processes. Over time, knowledge processes will be managed with greater and greater rigor. It will be in everyone's best interest.

Be Proactive

The next basic rule for managing your reputation is to be proactive. That means communicating early and often about what you do and how you do it. There are a number of channels of communication with stakeholders—and the number grows every day. Corporate communications, marketing, and, really, every client-facing staff person is part of this communication process.

In this discussion, it is important to make a distinction between your reputation and your brand. They are related but have some important differences. Up to this point, we have actually talked a number of times about brand as an asset of your organization. Brands are part of the relationship capital of your organization. Brand is usually associated with a product or service, so by definition, it is something that you create and build. You can actually protect your brand legally. You invest in trying to influence how people understand your brand through activities such as advertising. Ultimately, you have a lot to say about how your brand is defined and how it is perceived in the marketplace.

Your brand can affect your reputation. But reputation encompasses much more than that. As we have said, it is the sum total of your entire organization. Although everything you do as an organization influences your reputation, it is ultimately external stakeholders that will give you the thumbs up or down. You should try to help your stakeholders understand the important factors of your operation to support your reputation. But there is less room for the kind of artful and creative communication that marks good brand building. With reputation, you need to let the facts speak for themselves. The best protection against unexpected challenges to your reputation is consistent and proactive communication. Build and protect your reputation by providing good information about your operations—tangible and intangible—on an ongoing basis.

Be Transparent

We recently worked with Nick Shepherd on a paper for the Institute of Management Accounting on intangibles reporting. We undertook this paper together because we shared a belief with Nick that there will be significant changes in the reporting of intangibles in coming years. Nick helped us see the historical context to this trend. The current reporting paradigms were created in the aftermath of the Great Depression. Prior to that time, shareholders in a company did not have access to its financial statements. When new reporting requirements made this mandatory, they were met with all kinds of resistance and fear. Yet, today, we cannot imagine making an investment without this basic information.

We see new changes coming in reporting. The reason why was put very succinctly by former SEC Chairman Cox a few years ago:

> At a time when we have 24-hour news—and even 24-hour pizza delivery—why are we still living by the 10-K and the 10-Q? If investors are going to be responsible for the growth of their investments, for picking which funds to put into their 401(k) nest eggs, they'll need user-friendly, responsive numbers that are easily accessible.[6]

What will be the driver of this change? Will it be a top-down imposition of new reporting standards by a governmental agency? We do not believe so. That's so industrial era. We believe, we hope, that it will be a bottom-up movement from stakeholders like investors, analysts, bankers, boards of directors, and even managers: stakeholders who will want to understand the full picture of what is really going on in a company; stakeholders who know that a knowledge-dependent company should be able to describe and measure the knowledge side of its business.

THE TOYOTA CASE

As this book goes to press, Toyota is facing a severe reputational crisis. It appears that the company broke all three of these rules for managing its reputation. First of all, it made one or more mistakes that led to deaths and accidents. Secondly, it failed to be proactive about addressing the mistake(s), which was especially surprising to the public given the company's long-time reputation for continuous improvement and quality. Thirdly, it failed to be transparent and tried to push the problem off for too long.

This crisis will be analyzed in greater detail in the future but one thing is clear: the company's famed empowerment of employees to solve problems seemed to reach a barrier somewhere at the top of the org chart. The knowledge flow and learning from the bottom up and the outside in that we have talked about so much in this book was blocked by an over-confident management team that was struggling to manage growth that effectively doubled the company's manufacturing capacity in the decade of the 2000's. The extent of the reaction to the company's mistake(s) was probably increased by the high esteem with which the company was held in the past. Toyota is not the first to make a mistake, nor will they be the last. But this example shows that it's not the mistake that gets you in trouble. It's how you handle it.

WHAT INFORMATION SHOULD BE COMMUNICATED TO STAKEHOLDERS?

Where to start? What should be communicated? If you have been doing the exercises in this book, you already have a great start on developing a helpful information set for your stakeholders. The following list is included for your reference but for more detail, please refer back to Chapter 9 and the applicable discussion in earlier chapters.

1. Intangibles inventory—What are your key competencies, relationships, processes, and intellectual property?
2. Knowledge factory model—How does it all fit together to create value for your customers?
3. Investment—What did it cost to build your knowledge factory? What does it cost to maintain it and operate it?

4. Assessment and operational performance data—What are your data telling you about the functioning of your knowledge factory? Although you don't have to share operational data, you should share what you are learning from it.
5. Strategy—How does all this information relate to your strategy and business opportunity?
6. Key performance indicators—What are the key indicators that you are watching? What trends do they show?

Of course, as we explained in the earlier chapters of Part III, most companies are just focusing (internally and externally) on key performance indicators. This kind of dashboard approach is fine until one of the indicators turns red. That's the wrong moment to open the hood and take a look at all the parts of your knowledge factory that affect that indicator. If you want to get it right, don't rely on key performance indicators (KPIs) without backing them up with a disciplined process of inventory, investment, assessment, and strategy.

THE COLOPLAST EXPERIMENT

Here is a simple example of the value of greater transparency. This experiment was performed by PricewaterhouseCoopers' (PwC) Corporate Reporting practice a number of years ago. It used two versions of an annual report from Coloplast, a Danish company recognized as a leader in corporate reporting:

- The first was an original version of the Coloplast annual report. In addition to the normal information in an average annual report (financial statements, narrative, and a few key metrics), this report included extensive *quantified nonfinancial indicators* that made a clear link between its strategy and its financial performance.
- The second version of the report stripped out the quantified nonfinancial indicators data. The stripped-down report was still richer in detail than the annual reports provided by most companies in the market. But the critical nonfinancial indicators were missing.

Two groups of analysts reviewed the different reports. The conclusions were striking. The full report led the analysts to come up with a much more consistent estimate of future revenue and earnings than the analysts who had the modified report although, interestingly, the average estimate was lower for the full-report analysts than for the modified-report analysts. But the estimate differences belied the overall recommendation made by the two groups of analysts: 60 percent of full-report analysts actually gave a "buy" recommendation for the company while 80 percent of the modified-report analysts gave the stock a "sell" recommendation.[7]

This study reinforces the message of all the academic studies referenced in Chapter 7 that the markets see value in intangibles and that better information leads to better valuation. The advantage that this study has over the others is that it included a full set of data that put context around the entire operation rather than just one expense category such as research and development or marketing. It is sobering to think of the very different consequences that a company would face based on the vastly different recommendations of the two analyst groups—differences that would affect share price, reputation, and overall value of a company.

Yet, the results of this study are not surprising. Everyone knows intuitively that information about intangibles is important and valuable. They just don't know where to start. Hopefully, you are beginning to get mad. There is something wrong with our system.

WHY ISN'T SOMEONE DOING SOMETHING?

So we know that you are asking why more isn't being done. There are actually a lot of top-down initiatives trying to promote the ideas of intangible capital and enhanced business reporting.

In the area of corporate reporting, there have been a number of initiatives. The latest in the United States is called Enhanced Business Reporting (EBR 360). This is a consortium whose founding members include the American Institute of Certified Public Accountants, Grant Thornton LLP, Microsoft Corporation, and PwC. Each of these members contributed a six-figure sum to the effort. It is the ultimate in a top-down organization. Having said that, they created a starting framework that reflects the key components of intangible capital.

EBR 360 in turn is one of the founding members of the World Intellectual Capital Initiative (WICI) which also includes the European Federation of Financial Analyst Societies; Japan Ministry of Economy, Trade and Industry; Organization for Economic Development and Cooperation; Society for Knowledge Economics; University of Ferrara; and Waseda University. The European Commission participates in the WICI as an observer. The stated purpose of the initiative is to create a "global framework for measuring and reporting on intellectual assets and capital." PwC, among others, has contributed some of its corporate reporting materials to the effort.

There are also many national programs in Europe and Asia focused on teaching companies how to leverage intangible capital for growth and innovation. Each of these has its own framework, which is a little bit of overkill. To date, there is no equivalent program in the United States. We have mixed feelings about that. On the one hand, we obviously would like to see more attention to this subject. On the other hand, we are not convinced that the challenges of intangibles measurement and management can be solved from the top down.

These initiatives are good. But they are not going to change the world. You are going to change the world. Actually, you are going to change your company. And someone else is going to change their company. Not because you have to but because it is in your company's interest to do so to:

- Grow faster
- Attract better employees and partners
- Get financing from your bankers
- Get a better valuation from the stock market, private investors, or a merger partner

We believe that new standards for corporate reporting and reputation will be built from the bottom up this time.

CONCLUSION: WHY DON'T YOU DO SOMETHING?

You have heard us say throughout the book that intangibles measurement and management is not something that needs to wait for direction from on high. You can start identifying, managing, and measuring your intangibles today. You don't need to create full reports for immediate release to the market. Just start by thinking about what your knowledge factory looks like. What are the key networks inside the factory? How can they be managed for maximum innovation and growth? What kind of information do you need to make the right decisions? It is all within your reach. The only thing standing between you and a change is, well, you.

This is frankly one of our major reasons for writing this book: To foment a revolution; to empower managers and employees and external stakeholders to ask the right questions, produce better information, and use knowledge to get busy. There is a world of challenges facing our society—and each represents an opportunity for growth. Every industry can and will be re-created in a new knowledge-era form. Someone else will try it. The only question is whether you will beat them to it.

EXERCISE

Does your reputation give your organization a license to continue to do business?

- What is the overall state of your reputation?
- What are the key drivers of the reputation?
- Are there misperceptions that influence it?
- Will your reputation support where you want to go in the coming years?

You can download a worksheet for this exercise at www.intangiblecapitalbook.com.

|c|o|n|c||l|u|s|i|o|n|

In the 1960s, there was a popular television show in the United States called *The Beverly Hillbillies*. Each week, the show opened with a theme song that told the story of a man named Jed Clampett. On the screen, you saw a poorly dressed man running across a meadow, raising his rifle, shooting at but missing his elusive prey. Then the camera zoomed in on a black substance bubbling up from the ground. Clampett's bullet had struck oil. He packed up his family and moved to Beverly Hills, an accidental millionaire.

What's the difference between Jed Clampett and you? It's that you already know there is oil under your feet. Your business has significant reserves of knowledge, the new oil of our economy. Put to work in the right way, this knowledge has the potential to make your company very successful. But you may be more like Clampett than you may care to admit. You probably work at a fast pace. You may have never stopped to think about what the knowledge economy means to your business. You may be relying more on luck and intuition rather than disciplined management to exploit the reserves of knowledge hidden inside your organization. It's time to change all that. It's time to reap the benefits of intangibles management.

PERFORMANCE
Seeing the intangible side of your business as the New Factory will help you to understand and optimize its performance. In Part I, you learned how to identify the components of the knowledge factory—human, relationship, and structural capital—how to get paid for them, and how to unleash their infinite power through the right combination, the right business model. You learned how to build an inventory and a model of this factory. You learned that the real promise of the factory comes when human and relationship capital are combined with structural capital, the knowledge that is captured in your company and converted into a re-usable, scalable form. It is through structural capital that you can experience (and profit from) the infinite potential of structural knowledge—and optimize the performance of your business.

INNOVATION
The nature of a business built on knowledge requires New Management that can do more than execute strategy; it must also fuel innovation. In Part II you learned that the hierarchical organization structure that was ideal for the industrial era limits the potential of your business in the knowledge era.

When the success of your business relies on the knowledge of your people, your customers, and partners of all kinds, you need knowledge to flow from the bottom up and outside in. You need to think of your organization in terms of a series of collaborative networks, not just a pyramid-shaped organization chart. You need to take a fundamentally different approach to strategic management: you cannot just rely on setting a course and executing single-mindedly; you also need to build in a way to leverage the knowledge of your organization's intangibles—human, relationship, and structural capital—to find new opportunities, explore new courses, and fuel innovation for your business.

VALUATION

Creating a New Accounting system for intangibles will support your management and also help you maximize the valuation you receive from the market. In Part III you learned that, despite what your accountants may tell you, the money invested in building the knowledge factories of businesses around the world has been considerable and is very real. It is in your interest to add up how much you really invest each year in this intangible capital expenditure. Use that data the way that you would any financial data to measure the return and results your company is reaping from the investment.

But remember that financial data alone are insufficient to describe the workings of the knowledge factory. The other two kinds of information you will need include assessments and indicators. Combined together, these three kinds of data—investment, assessment, and indicators—will enable you to triangulate the current and future earnings potential of your business. This information is important on its own as an input to the management of your company. But it is also critical to external stakeholders: analysts, investors, bankers, and potential merger partners. They will use it to evaluate and value your company as a whole.

REPUTATION

Doing it all well and communicating your process clearly will ensure that you build and maintain a good reputation. In the final chapter of this book, you learned that reputation is more important than ever because the knowledge-era organization does not own two of its key sources of knowledge: human and relationship capital. A knowledge factory will not work without these inputs. Yet employees and partners cannot be forced to contribute. They are not machines that can be bolted to the floor. You have to maintain a reputation that motivates them to stay connected with you. A good reputation in the eyes of your stakeholders is your license to continue to do business in the future. A good reputation is earned by the way that you manage and measure your intangible capital—and how well you communicate this to stakeholders. Every company today is much more vulnerable to reputational crises precisely because they are not using sound intangibles management tools and practices.

Performance. Innovation. Valuation. Reputation. These should be reasons enough to get serious about intangibles management. But don't forget the historic moment. The industrial model is breaking down across our economy. Energy production and use, transportation, construction, manufacturing, health care, food production, and education all need to be re-created in a sustainable, knowledge-era form. These changes will roll through our economy and create opportunities for just about every business.

How will you rise to these opportunities? By building brick-and-mortar factories? By building fully integrated businesses that "do it all"? No, you will do it by hiring a core of knowledgeable employees. By cultivating strong partners. By taking advantage of information technology to build structural capital. By creating solutions to solve your customers' problems. By looking for new places to apply your existing knowledge. By finding new ways to provide services as well as build products. You will rise to these opportunities by becoming an intangible capitalist.

The New Factory, the New Management, the New Accounting—these are the tools of the intangible capitalist. They will help you optimize the performance, innovation, valuation, and reputation of your organization. You can get started right away using the exercises at the end of each chapter. This book and these exercises have the potential to unlock millions of dollars in improvements in your organization.

But remember what you learned in Chapter 1. Books and worksheets are low-value knowledge products. They inform but they do not resolve. We have helped show you the way and hope to help you by creating a conversation and posting more tools on-line at www.intangiblecapitalbook.com. But the real value will be created when this knowledge is put to work inside your organization. The ideal people to put this knowledge to work are you and your colleagues. You know your own company. You just need to learn to see it in a new way. Follow the steps outlined in the exercises starting with identifying and modeling your knowledge factory all the way through creating an intangibles data set. If you follow these steps, you will become intangible capitalists. You will learn to make the most of the hidden but gigantic potential that is already there, inside your company, waiting to be tapped. You will solve new problems and profit while doing it.

Now it's up to you. Our only question is: *What are you waiting for?*

CHAPTER 1

1. Paul Romer, "The Soft Revolution: Achieving Growth by Managing Intangibles," in *Intangible Assets: Values, Measures, and Risks*, eds. John R. M. Hand and Baruch Lev, (Oxford: Oxford University Press, 2003), 67–71.
2. Steven Piersanti, "The 10 Awful Truths about Book Publishing," accessed at http://www.bkpextranet.com/10awfultruths.pdf.
3. David Ruder, "Finessing Finance with Brand Assets" (presented to the Intangible Asset Finance Society via telephone conference in March 2009), available at http://iafinance.org/_literature_38820/Trademarks_-_RPX_Corp_09-Mar-06.
4. David Hetzel, "Patent Monetization" (presented to the Intangible Asset Finance Society via teleconference in December 2008), available at http://iafinance.org/_literature_31948/Patent-Motorola-08-Dec-5.
5. Nicholas G. Carr, "The End of Corporate Reporting," *MITSloan Management Review,* Spring 2005.
6. Michael Fitzgerald, "X Woman," *Condé Nast Portfolio*, October 2008: 163.
7. Jonathan Schwartz, "Sun's Network Innovations 3 of 4," *Jonathan's Blog* (March 11, 2009), available at http://blogs.sun.com/jonathan/entry/commercial_innovation_3_of_4.

CHAPTER 2

1. Michael Porter, *Competitive Advantage* (New York: The Free Press, 1985), 37.
2. Alex Edmans, "Does the Stock Market Fully Value Intangibles? Employee Satisfaction and Equity Prices," August 13, 2009, accessed at http://papers.ssrn.com/sol3/papers.cfm?abstract_id=985735.
3. Noam Cohen, "Care to Write Army Doctrine? With ID, Log On," *New York Times*, August 13, 2009. Available at http://www.nytimes.com/2009/08/14/business/14army.html?_r=1&th&emc=th.
4. Steven Mains and Laura W. Geller, "Freeing Ideas from Their Silos," *strategy + business*, February 12, 2008, available at http://www.strategy-business.com/li/leadingideas/li00062.
5. Robert Rittereiser, "Imposing Performance (Behavioral) Requirements on a Commercial Partner" (presentation to the Intangible Asset Finance Society in April 2009), available at http://iafinance.org/events (data from comments in the recording, not the slides).

6. Irving Wladawsky-Berger, "On the Transition from the Industrial to the Knowledge Economy" (presentation at the U.S. National Academies conference on *Intangible Assets: Measuring and Enhancing Their Contribution to Corporate Value and Economic Growth*, June 23, 2008). Available at http://sites.nationalacademies.org/PGA/step/IntangibleAssets/PGA_046311.

CHAPTER 3

1. Mary Adams, "You Can Grow like Google," at http://www.youtube.com/watch?v=brBwWqiSg8g.

CHAPTER 4

1. Thomas Wailgum, "45 Years of Wal-Mart History: A Technology Time Line," *CIO Magazine*, October 17, 2007, http://www.cio.com/article/147005/45_Years_of_Wal_Mart_History_A_Technology_Time_Line, accessed on August 18, 2009.
2. Peter F. Drucker, *Managing in the Next Society* (New York: St. Martin's Press, 2002), Chapter 1.
3. Verna Allee, *The Future of Knowledge: Increasing Prosperity through Value Networks* (Oxford: Butterworth-Heinemann/Elsevier: 2003), Chapters 12 and 13. Information also available at www.valuenetworks.org and www.valuenetworks.com.
4. Rob Cross, Andrew Parker, Laurence Prusak, and Stephen P. Borgatti, "Knowing What We Know: Supporting Knowledge Creation and Sharing in Social Networks," *Ageless Learner,* http://agelesslearner.com/articles/knowing_crossetal_tc600.html.
5. Thomas Eisenmann, Geoffrey Parker, and Marshall W. Van Alstyne, "Strategies for Two-Sided Markets," *Harvard Business Review*, October 2006: 92.
6. Jane Wei-Skillern and Sonia Marciano, "The Networked Nonprofit," *Stanford Social Innovation Review*, Spring 2008: 38–39.
7. Ken Jarboe, "The Machine versus the Virus," *The Intangible Economy* blog. November 8, 2007, available at http://www.athenaalliance.org/weblog/archives/2007/11/the_machine_ver.html.
8. "Mobilizing Human Capital," *Consulting*, March/April 2006: 17–18.
9. Christopher Meyer, "The Best Networks Are Really Worknets," *Harvard Business Review*, February 2007: 47–48.

CHAPTER 5

1. Peter F. Drucker, *Managing in the Next Society* (New York: Truman Talley Books, St. Martin's Press, 2002), 125.
2. We first read about this in Tammy Erickson, "Straight from Hollywood: The Project-Based Workforce," *Across the Ages* blog, January 29, 2008, http://blogs.harvardbusiness.org/erickson/2008/01/straight_from_hollywood_the_pr.html. The concept is attributed to a number of people including Charles Handy, *The Age of Unreason* (Cambridge: Harvard Business School Press, 1990).

3. *The First Measured Century*, PBS on-line book, Chapter 2.1, "Men's Occupations," available at http://www.pbs.org/fmc/book/2work1.htm.
4. Jeffry Krasner, "Beth Israel Finds Cure for Layoffs," *Boston Globe*, March 20, 2009, accessed at http://www.boston.com/business/healthcare/articles/2009/03/20/beth_israel_finds_cure_for_layoffs/.
5. "Weekend Workout: Not a Cure All, but Creativity Is Saving Some Jobs," *Globe and Mail*, January 25, 2009.
6. Nicholas G. Carr, "The End of Corporate Computing," *MIT Sloan Management Review*, Spring 2005.
7. Ellen McGirt, "How Cisco's CEO John Chambers Is Turning the Tech Giant Socialist," *Fast Company*, December 2008/January 2009, also available at http://www.fastcompany.com/magazine/131/revolution-in-san-jose.html.
8. Henry Blodget, "Has Cisco's John Chambers Lost His Mind?" *Silicon Valley Insider* blog, August 6, 2009, available at http://www.businessinsider.com/henry-blodget-has-ciscos-john-chambers-lost-his-mind-2009-8.
9. Marshall Krantz, "Who Needs a COO?" *CFO*, August 1, 2008, available at http://www.cfo.com/article.cfm/11871792?f=alerts.

CHAPTER 6

1. Mohanbir Sawhney, Robert C. Wolcott, and Inigo Arroniz, "The 12 Different Ways for Companies to Innovate," *MIT Sloan Management Review* (Spring 2006): 75–81.
2. Debra Amidon, "The Triple Knowledge Lens," available at http://www.inthekzone.com/kIZ-triplelens.htm.
3. Henry Mintzberg, *The Rise and Fall of Strategic Planning: Reconceiving Roles for Planning, Plans, Planners* (New York: The Free Press, 1994), 24.
4. "Cultivating Innovation: Lessons from America's Chief Innovation Officers," white paper by Mary Adams, available at http://www.i-capitaladvisors.com/wp-content/uploads/2009/02/white-paper-cultivating-innovation-20081.pdf.
5. Bala Iyer and Thomas H. Davenport, "Reverse Engineering Google's Innovation Machine," *Harvard Business Review*, April 2008: 64.

CHAPTER 7

1. L.C. Hunter, Elizabeth Webster, and Anne Wyatt, "Measuring Intangible Investment," Melbourne Institute Working Paper Series, 15/05, available at http://www.google.com/url?sa=t&source=web&ct=res&cd=1&url=http%3A%2F%2Fwww.melbourneinstitute.com%2Fwp%2Fwp2009n12.pdf&ei=082WSq_MLdCYlAeomrSvDA&rct=j&q=%22measuring+intangible+investment%22+melbourne&usg=AFQjCNF29GIc5fFs4TUgQ28OdASLgXcq6g.
2. Leonard Nakamura, "A Trillion Dollars a Year in Intangible Investment and the New Economy," in *Intangible Assets: Values, Measures and Risks*, eds. John Hand and Baruch Lev (Oxford: Oxford University Press, 2003), 25–28.
3. Carol A. Corrado, Charles R. Hulten, and Daniel E. Sichel, "Intangible Capital and Economic Growth," *Finance and Economics Discussion*

Series, Divisions of Research & Statistics and Monetary Affairs, Federal Reserve Board, 2006, 24.

4. Michael Mandel, "The GDP Mirage," *BusinessWeek*, October 29, 2009.

5. Ernst & Young, "Acquisition Accounting: What's Next for You," February 2009, available at http://int.sitestat.com/ernst-and-young/international/s?TAS_Acquisition_accounting_Whats_next_for_you&ns_type=pdf&ns_url=%5bhttp://www.ey.com/Global/assets.nsf/International/TAS_Acquisition_accounting_Whats_next_for_you/$file/TAS_Acquisition_accounting_Whats_next_for_you.pdf%5d.

6. Umair Haque, "How to Be a 21st Century Capitalist," *Edge Economy* blog, December 3, 2008. Available at http://blogs.harvardbusiness.org/haque/2008/12/how_to_be_a_21st_century_capit.html.

7. L.C. Hunter, Elizabeth Webster, and Anne Wyatt, "Identifying Corporate Expenditures on Intangibles Using GAAP," draft paper provided by the authors.

8. Many thanks to Michael D. Kimbrough at the Harvard Business School who helped us with a review of relevant research as well as supplying his (at the time) unpublished paper written with Leigh McAlister, "Commentaries and Rejoinder to 'Marketing and Firm Value: Metrics, Methods, Findings and Future Directions.'" Later published in the *Journal of Marketing Research* XLVI (June 2009).

9. David Aboody and Baruch Lev, "The Value Relevance of Intangibles: The Case of Software Capitalization," *Journal of Accounting Research* 36, Studies on Enhancing the Financial Reporting Model (1998): 161–191.

10. Emad Mohd, "Accounting for Software Development and Information Asymmetry," *The Accounting Review* 80 no. 4 (2005): 1211–1231.

11. Baruch Lev and Theodore Sougiannis, "The Capitalization, Amortization and Value-Relevance of R&D," *Journal of Accounting and Economics* 21 (1996): 107–138.

12. Christopher D. Ittner and David F. Larcker, "Are Non-Financial Measures Leading Indicators of Financial Performance? An Analysis of Customer Satisfaction," *Journal of Accounting Research* 36 Supplement (1998): 1–46.

13. David Aboody and Baruch Lev, "Information Asymmetry, R&D, and Insider Gains," *Journal of Finance* 55, no. 6 (2000): 2747–2766.

14. Michael D. Kimbrough, "The Influences of Financial Statement Recognition and Analyst Coverage on the Market's Valuation of R&D Capital," *The Accounting Review* 82 (October 2007): 1195–1225.

15. Louis K. C. Chan, Josef Lakonishok, and Theodore Sougiannis, "The Stock Market Valuation of Research and Development Expenditures," *Journal of Finance* 56, no. 6 (December 2001): 2431–2456.

16. Jeff P. Boone and K. K. Raman, "Balance Sheet R&D Assets and Market Liquidity," *Journal of Accounting and Public Policy* 20 (2001): 97–128.

17. Michael D. Kimbrough, "The Effect of Conference Calls on Analyst and Market Underreaction to Earnings Announcements," *The Accounting Review* 80 (January 2005): 189–219.

18. Brian J. Bushee, "The Influence of Institutional Investors on Myopic R&D Investment Behavior," *The Accounting Review* 7303 (1998): 305–333.
19. John R. Graham, Campbell R. Harvey, and Shiva Rajgopal, "The Economic Implications of Corporate Financial Reporting," *Journal of Accounting and Economics* 40 (December 2005): 3–73.

CHAPTER 8

1. Umair Haque, "How to Be a 21st Century Capitalist," *Edge Economy* blog, December 3, 2008, available at http://blogs.harvardbusiness.org/haque/2008/12/how_to_be_a_21st_century_capit.html.
2. "2th Annual Global CEO Survey—What Matters to CEOs in 2009?" PricewaterhouseCoopers, available at http://www.pwc.co.uk/eng/issues/ceomatters.html.
3. A great source on all the available open solutions is the white paper by Kenan Patrick Jarboe, "Measuring Intangibles, A Summary of Recent Activity," Athena Institute (April 2007), available at http://www.athenaalliance.org/apapers/MeasuringIntangibles.htm.
4. The phrase "disruptive innovation" was coined by Clay Christenson to describe innovations that enter a market at the low end but eventually challenge the market incumbents.
5. Mary Adams and Peder Hofman-Bang, "The Weakest Link in Corporate IAM," *Intangible Assets Management Magazine* 35 (May/June 2009): 65–70.
6. Mary Adams and Henrik Martin, "IC: Ready to Cross the Chasm?" paper presented to the European Conference on Intellectual Capital (April 2009). Paper available at http://www.i-capitaladvisors.com/wp-content/uploads/2009/05/ecic-ic-ready-to-cross-the-chasm.pdf.

CHAPTER 9

1. Ian Graham, "What's Wrong with Targets?" *Perspectives on Performance* 6, no. 1: 15–18.
2. Christopher Shea, "Did Clemson Game the U.S. News Rankings?" *Brainiac* blog, June 3, 2009, available at http://www.boston.com/bostonglobe/ideas/brainiac/2009/06/did_clemson_gam.html.
3. Daniel Pink, "The Surprising Science of Motivation," A Taste of TED Global 2009, available at http://www.ted.com/talks/dan_pink_on_motivation.html.
4. For a thought-provoking comparison of these two points, please see: J. Mourtisen, H. Thorsgaard Larsen, and P. N. Bukh, "Dealing with the Knowledge Economy: Intellectual Capital versus Balanced Scorecard," *Journal of Intellectual Capital* 6-1 (2005), 8–27.
5. Jeff Jarvis, "Dell Learns to Listen," *BusinessWeek*, October 17, 2007, accessed at http://www.businessweek.com/bwdaily/dnflash/content/oct2007/db20071017_277576.htm.

6. Lowell L. Bryan and Claudia L. Joyce, *Mobilizing Minds: Creating Wealth from Talent in the 21st Century Organization* (New York: McGraw Hill, 2007), 5–11.

7. F.F. Reichheld, "The One Number You Need to Grow," *Harvard Business Review* 81, no. 12 (December 2003): 46–54.

8. Timothy L. Keiningham, Lerzan Aksoy, Bruce Cooil, and Tor Wallin Andreassen, "Linking Customer Loyalty to Growth," *MIT Sloan Management Review* (Summer 2008): 51–57.

9. PwC, "Value Analysis Statement," available at http://pwc.blogs.com/corporatereporting/files/value_analysis_statement.pdf. The system is also explained in greater detail in *The New Capitalists*, written by Stephen Davis, Jon Lukomnik, and David Pitt-Watson (Boston: Harvard Business Press, 2006), 170.

CHAPTER 10

1. Peter F. Drucker, *The Essential Drucker* (New York: HarperCollins, 2001), 111.

2. Francesco Guerrera, "Welch Condemns Share Price Focus," *Financial Times* (March 12, 2009), available at http://www.ft.com/cms/s/0/294ff1f2-0f27-11de-ba10-0000779fd2ac,dwp_uuid=c770f55e-0fac-11de-a8ae-0000779fd2ac.html?ftcamp=rss&nclick_check=1.

3. The Aspen Institute, "Overcoming Short-termism: A Call for a More Responsible Approach to Investment and Business Management" (September 9, 2009), available at http://www.aspeninstitute.org/sites/default/files/content/docs/business%20and%20society%20program/overcome_short_state0909.pdf.

4. Scott Leibs, "View on Sustainability Reporting," *CFO* (December 2007): 63–66.

5. See www.unglobalcompact.org.

6. Christopher Cox, "The Interactive Data Revolution: Improved Disclosure for Investors, Less Expensive Reporting for Companies" (speech to the American Enterprise Institute, Washington, DC, on May 30, 2006). Accessed at http://www.sec.gov/news/speech/2006/spch053006cc.htm.

7. "The Coloplast Experiment," PricewaterhouseCoopers, available at http://www.corporatereporting.com/benefits-reporting.html.

index

About the Authors

MARY ADAMS is a co-founder of I-Capital Advisors and Trek Consulting. She is one of the leading U.S. experts on intangible capital. She is the author of the *Smarter Companies* blog and the creator of the *IC Knowledge Center*, an on-line community with open resources and discussions about intangible capital. Prior to starting her consulting business, she had a 15-year career as a high-risk lender at Citicorp and Sanwa Business Credit.

MICHAEL OLEKSAK is a co-founder of the Exit Planning Exchange and Trek Consulting. He has been a trusted advisor to countless owners/managers of middle market businesses, helping them to improve the performance and value of their companies. Prior to co-founding Trek in 2002, Michael built a Latin American business for the PORTIA software group at Thomson Financial. He began his career as a Vice President and commercial lender for Bank of Boston.

Mary and Michael met in the Dominican Republic in 1984 while working for U.S. banks and later transferred to Los Angeles. Early in their marriage, they co-authored the breakthrough book, *Beisbol: Latin Americans and the Grand Old Game.* They have two teenage sons and live in Winchester, MA.